R E A L
intimacy

A Couple's Guide

to **Healthy**,

Genuine

Sexuality

Kristin B. Hodson, MSW,LCSW
Alisha B. Worthington, BSW, SSW
with Thomas G. Harrison, MSW, LCSW

REAL *intimacy*

A Couple's Guide

to **Healthy,**

Genuine

Sexuality

Kristin B. Hodson, MSW, LCSW
Alisha B. Worthington, BSW, SSW
with Thomas G. Harrison, MSW, LCSW

CFI
An Imprint of Cedar Fort, Inc.
Springville, Utah

AUTHORS' NOTE: All names* used in *Real Intimacy: A Couple's Guide to Healthy, Genuine Sexuality* have been changed. If any name used is similar to a circumstance, it is purely coincidental.
*except in the case of Loralee and David's story in "First Encounters"

© 2012 Kristin B. Hodson, Alisha B. Worthington, Thomas G. Harrison
All rights reserved.

No part of this book may be reproduced in any form whatsoever, whether by graphic, visual, electronic, film, microfilm, tape recording, or any other means, without prior written permission of the publisher, except in the case of brief passages embodied in critical reviews and articles.

This is not an official publication of The Church of Jesus Christ of Latter-day Saints. The opinions and views expressed herein belong solely to the authors and do not necessarily represent the opinions or views of Cedar Fort, Inc. Permission for the use of sources, graphics, and photos is also solely the responsibility of the authors.

ISBN 13: 978-1-4621-1052-0

Published by CFI, an imprint of Cedar Fort, Inc., 2373 W. 700 S., Springville, UT 84663
Distributed by Cedar Fort, Inc., www.cedarfort.com

LIBRARY OF CONGRESS CATALOGING-IN-PUBLICATION DATA

Harrison, Thomas G., 1949- author.
Real intimacy / Thomas G. Harrison, MSW, LCSW, Kristin B. Hodson, MSW, LCSW, Alisha B. Worthington, BSW, SSW.
    pages cm
  Includes bibliographical references.
  ISBN 978-1-4621-1052-0 (alk. paper)
  1. Sex--Religious aspects--Church of Jesus Christ of Latter-day Saints. 2. Sexual ethics. 3. Married people--Sexual behavior. 4. Marriage--Religious aspects--Church of Jesus Christ of Latter-day Saints. 5. Church of Jesus Christ of Latter-day Saints--Doctrines. I. Hodson, Kristin B., 1980- author. II. Worthington, Alisha B., 1972- author. III. Title.

  BX8643.S49H37 2012
  248.8'44--dc23

                        2012015655

Cover design by Brian Halley
Cover design © 2012 by Lyle Mortimer
Edited and typeset by Emily S. Chambers

Printed in the United States of America

10 9 8 7 6 5 4 3 2 1

Printed on acid-free paper

CONTENTS

Contents

FOREWORD

"I JUST WANT TO HAVE A REAL DISCUSSION ABOUT SEX AND INTI-
macy." That desperate plea—voiced by many of their clients—
prompted Kristin B. Hodson, Alisha B. Worthington, and Thomas
G. Harrison to produce this long-overdue book. It certainly is a real
discussion about how to find real intimacy—sexual and otherwise—
with our spouses. With unembarrassed candor, *Real Intimacy* features
straightforward discussions that help married couples overcome attitudes and barriers to the "oneness" they desperately want and need.

Early on, *Real Intimacy* hits us between the eyes with the sad truth:
Most of us enter married life with little or no idea of what "real intimacy" means, much less how to develop it. Parents and friends dance
around the concept, giving us a distorted view that intimacy occurs
naturally with enough romps in the sack. After the wedding, we're
sent off to grope in the dark—literally and figuratively—in a clueless
process that can produce pain and ultimately destroy intimacy. This
book is a must-read for both the soon-to-be married and for veteran-
married couples who want to finally find or re-kindle "real intimacy."

Real Intimacy explains that sex is one of four cornerstones of the
"pyramid of intimacy"—and it can be joyous and fun! This book is
filled with information that takes the mystery and ignorance out of

human sexual relationships. There's even a "Sex Ed 101" section to help us understand basic anatomy and techniques. But sex must be intertwined with other pyramid cornerstones—emotional, spiritual, and physical—to become great sex; and great sex deepens the other forms of intimacy in a divine circular process.

Real Intimacy is a joy to read, with creative and humor-filled analogies and suggestions for initiating discussions about potentially awkward or taboo topics like sexual responsiveness. "Approaching a conversation on intimacy with your spouse," the authors note, "can feel as potentially intimidating or daunting as your first sexual encounter. However, with a few basic skills . . . you will feel more confident and willing to begin having these conversations."

You know that this is not another timid, tepid book about sexuality and intimacy from a chapter title like "How Intimacy Is Like Dining." "When it comes to food, sometimes we want a seven-course meal, and sometimes we want a quick drive-through. Sometimes we are hungry and sometimes we are full—but we join our spouse anyway for a meal. Sometimes we don't feel hungry, but when we start eating we realize we were hungrier than we thought. Intimacy is the same way." Or how about a great discussion of one couple's use of the television characters—"Kermit and Miss Piggy"—to name their sexual regions.

I readily agreed to write the foreword for this wonderful book because I strongly endorse it and its refreshingly honest and candid approach. More important, I realized that it would bless the lives of so many good and wonderful people who are searching for real intimacy in their most treasured relationships.

—Matt Townsend
communication and relationship expert, talk show host

ACKNOWLEDGMENTS

THERE HAVE BEEN MANY PEOPLE WHO HAVE HELPED SHAPE this book, directly and indirectly through their various ways of involvement. We wanted to express our thanks specifically to Matt Townsend for your generosity and support, Natasha Parker for your time and support of this project, Tina Schermer Sellers for your thoughtful insight and valuable resource, Curt Burnett and Deanna Burnett for reading every word—editing along the way—and adding additional wisdom. Additionally, we want to thank the many individuals who have created valuable resources and made them accessible, and all of the people, clinicians, church leaders, and volunteers, working so hard to help individuals and couples everywhere feel healthy, happy, and a sense of normalcy. Above all, we give gratitude to a wise and loving Heavenly Father. Thank you.

—Kristin, Alisha, and Thom

TO MY FAMILY, FRIENDS, AND MENTORS, WHO HAVE BEEN supportive and believed in me while giving critical perspective to keep me in check and on track. To those in my past who have helped shaped me and give me priceless experiences. To my Mom who instilled in me the question, what's the worst that could happen?

To my Dad, who has always been a personal champion. To Thom and Alisha—what a blessing to be able to go through life's journey with you. To my husband, Jake, who stands by me and strives with a spirit of willingness to grow with me. To the "little" loves in my life, who embrace a mom who passionately lives out loud. I love you to the moon and back.

—**Kristin**

To my friends and family, who have cheered me on, supported me, and stuck with me through whatever adventure I decide to go on. To my parents, who created an environment in which any question could be asked and discussed—look what happened! To my children and their future spouses—may you have "real intimacy." To Bret, who is willing to walk this journey with me—"It's our deal."

—**Alisha**

INTRODUCTION

How this book is going to change your relationship and your life for the better!

I JUST WANT TO HAVE A REAL DISCUSSION ABOUT SEX AND INTI-macy! I'm tired of skirting around the issue." We've heard this plea over and over. There seems to be a growing desire among members of The Church of Jesus Christ of Latter-day Saints, and those of other faiths, to truly understand sexuality and intimacy as they impact each of us in the reality of our experience. How do the words "intimacy" and "real" intertwine in our day-to-day experience? In today's info-intense world, and our burgeoning new century, all one has to do is a simple Internet search to access an overwhelming and incredible amount of information on everything you did and did not want to know about sexuality and intimacy.

There are so many voices and opinions and so much information, but not all of it is helpful. Some of it is even damaging and destructive. It can be difficult to discern and wade through what may be correct or incorrect, true or speculative. It often takes hours of hunting through information in order to find some little nugget. This book is different. It will actually provide information and guidance, not just from the professionals working in this area, but directly from those asking the questions and living through the intimate relationships that all of us are experiencing. In its pages you will find your own voice and learn to speak about intimacy; you will learn to think intimately and how to change your intimate life, which, perhaps, you have not known how to do up to this point.

Could You Run a Marathon without Any Training or Knowledge?

If you have ever trained to run a race or have known someone who has, you find out how necessary proper training and preparation are. You must know about nutrition, develop a training plan, learn correct technique, and talk with others who have run a race before. If an injury is sustained, such as a sprained ankle, you wouldn't expect to just keep running or not to seek medical help. When it comes to running a race, we don't give ourselves the expectation that we should know all there is to know and not *need* to seek out resources to learn. Yet when it comes to our relationships, oftentimes we have the expectation that we should already know how to be a husband or wife. We think that if we sustain a relationship "injury" or have a festering problem, we should keep going and "run through it," which can create bigger problems.

Naturally, we learn our model for marriage and relationships from the circumstances in which we are raised. With the divorce rate being approximately 50 percent, whether you are a member of The Church of Jesus Christ of Latter-day Saints or not, the expectation to "just know" how to have a healthy relationship, good communication, and functional intimacy is relatively unrealistic. We are okay with going to the doctor when we are sick, the dentist when we have a toothache, and a chiropractor when our back is out of alignment, and we are even comfortable with the idea of seeing these professionals for wellness checkups. Unfortunately, getting repair work for our relationships tends to have a negative stigma.

Perspective Can Change Everything!

A woman recently had the opportunity to jump out of an airplane for the first time. One of the things she remarked about was the perspective she gained on the earth itself and her place in it, seeing it from eighteen thousand feet. Perspective gained is truly a wonderful thing. It can melt anger, resolve pain and guilt, and remove fear from almost any situation. It seems that in the area of sexual intimacy, too many are lacking needed perspective. And by not being able to speak openly and honestly with yourself, your spouse, a trusted friend, counselor, or God, we never even get to see the view from the top of the hill let alone the view from eighteen thousand feet! Just imagine if Christopher Columbus had been able to gain that kind of perspective before his voyage across the oceans! Imagine what a little perspective and putting things into context could do for you and your relationship or the future relationship you hope to have.

Why You Won't See Many Quotes from LDS Church Leadership in This Book

Although we, the authors, are members of The Church of Jesus Christ of Latter-day Saints, we feel like the information we have to offer can cross all religious lines. The principles are the same for all human beings. We all have the same basic body structure, hormonal makeup, and desires placed in us by a loving Heavenly Father who wants us to experience intimacy as part of our mortal experience. That being said, you will not find many quotes from the Brethren. We believe that much of what the Brethren say is a blanket statement for the entire membership of the Church and doesn't necessarily pertain to individual members or couples. Therefore, there are times when statements made to smaller congregations, regarding sexuality, have then been passed around and taken as something for which they were never intended. We want to refrain from speaking for the Brethren and using their words out of context. We are just speaking as fellow children of God, occasionally referencing scriptures, trying to make sense of the world around us and the bodies we have been given. Our experience with sexuality and intimacy is varied, so you will get an outlook from many different angles and perspectives.

"Seek Ye Out of the Best Books . . ."

The guiding principles of marital and family relationships can be found in "The Proclamation on the Family." It provides general guidelines to help us progress within our familial relationships. However, the Church is a religious institution. Its focus is on sharing the gospel, redeeming the dead, perfecting the Saints, and caring for the needy mostly through various worship opportunities at local churches and temples and in class settings. It is not a science institution, an art academy, or business school. While underlying guiding gospel principles can be applied within every realm, there is room for scholarship and specialized learning outside the institution of the Church. We are counseled to seek continued education in order to progress financially, socially, mentally, and emotionally. Marriage is not something one just "knows how to do" on an intuitive level. More often than not we seek advice, read commentaries, talk to our friends, or listen to lectures about various aspects of marriage, hoping to improve and enhance our own spousal relationship.

Social science, of which we are a part, is a science that exists as a specialized science outside the Church arena. If it weren't a necessary and valid science, places such as LDS Family Services wouldn't exist. Bishops would handle all mental health concerns instead of referring elsewhere. The Church recognizes the need for individualized assistance, from time to time, beyond the capabilities of the local ecclesiastical leadership. Just as you wouldn't have your bishop perform your knee surgery, you also wouldn't have him try to treat all mental health concerns either—and he wouldn't want to.

Each Couple and Relationship Is Totally Unique and Should Be Treated as Such

The title of the book, *Real Intimacy*, came from the honest desire to have a frank and open discussion on this topic. This book is intended to be read alone or with your partner, in the protected space of your relationship. Every couple and individual have a unique set of qualities and traits that create very specific wants and needs. We hope you will take a deep breath and read the information presented without unease. The chapter topics in this book were carefully thought about as each significantly pertains to the world in which we find ourselves today. We present this book humbly and with gratitude for the lessons we have learned and the experiences that have been shared with us by hundreds of individuals and couples.

You will not find this to be a "how to" or a "10 steps" book, but a book that evokes conversation and thought with practical ideas you can implement in your own relationships. When it comes to the topic of marital intimacy, there are countless subtopics that could be addressed. Due to the aforementioned fact that each situation is different, we cannot possibly touch on every possible topic. You wouldn't want to read it and we couldn't write it! We have touched on the aspects we feel are important in this day and age, and we provide a comprehensive reading list at the end of the book that will offer more in-depth information on a particular subject.

How to Use This Book—This Is Important!

We have written this book with two readers in mind: the reader who wants the main gist of the material, or the "Nuts and Bolts," and the reader who wants more in-depth information with the topic. At the end of each chapter, you will find a summary that will hit the main points, so that if one of you is reading the whole book and the other only the main points, you can have meaningful conversation regarding your intimacy. Also, there are questions at the end of each chapter that will help guide you into conversation if you're unsure where to start.

You will also find that we use the word intimacy as an umbrella term for physical, emotional, sexual, and spiritual intimacy unless specifically noted.

While you can read the book from beginning to end, there is no need to necessarily read this book according to the chapter sequential order. You may find chapters that are particularly relevant to you or your relationship, so start there. We use several analogies throughout the book. If you find yourself picking through the chapters based on relevancy, be sure to check out at least the "Nuts and Bolts" summaries of the other chapters so you have context and understanding.

Our Hope

We hope you find at least one or two nuggets of information you can use to apply to yourself and your relationship in order to strengthen and enhance it. There may be some things within your relationship that have caused pain for a long time, or you may just be starting along the journey of marriage. You may be single, divorced, widowed, married for the second or third time, or in a forty-year marriage. Whatever the case, you are still evolving, learning, and growing. Relationships are one of the main things we will take with us from this life to the next. We will continue to work at, enjoy, find passion in, and feel sorrow in our various relationships. However, through the prophet Alma, the Great Counselor gives us the hope we need to continue.

> But if ye will nourish [your relationship], yea, nourish the tree as it beginneth to grow, by your faith with great diligence, and with patience, looking forward to the fruit thereof, it shall take root; and behold it shall be a tree springing up unto everlasting life.
>
> Then, my brethren [and sisters], ye shall reap the rewards of your faith, and your diligence, and patience, and long-suffering, waiting for the tree to bring forth fruit unto you. (Alma 32:41, 43)

1
WHAT IS INTIMACY?

*Understanding intimacy from a physical,
sexual, emotional, and spiritual perspective*

D O YOU REMEMBER YOUR PARENTS USING THE WORD "INTI-
mate" as you drew nearer to your wedding day and finding
yourself wondering just what that word truly meant? Gina
recalls older couples giving her winks, nudges, or knowing glances but
not actually explaining *anything* about the concept of marital intimacy.
It seemed to be this vague idea hanging out in the atmosphere without
a tether. And yet, after she was married and discovered the paradoxes
and complexities entailed in real intimacy, she found herself winking
and nodding at younger girls who were themselves about to be married.
Gina had the same difficulty trying to put this concept into words as
the older ones! She was glad to learn about this book in order to help
others have some usable knowledge instead of just a wink and a nod.
Just coming up with a working definition of "intimacy" is difficult.
Many books claiming to discuss intimacy focus mainly on either sex
alone, or on the emotional and spiritual aspect while neglecting the
physical component. We wanted to write a book that would cross
that bridge and actually seek a more holistic approach. Real intimacy
doesn't differentiate between physical, spiritual, sexual, and emotional
components. It combines them all.

Take a moment and think about what your definition is. Do you think it is the same for your partner? You may be surprised by what he or she says. Our culture seems to use the word "intimacy" to define any sort of physical connection. It can be confusing to hear someone remark about the intimate relationship she has with a sibling and yet also refer to "being intimate" with her partner over the weekend. Do they mean sexually or emotionally?

If you're married, think back to advice you were given, if any, before you were married concerning your impending honeymoon. Did anyone actually give you any usable information or did they just talk using vague phrases like, "Intimacy is important in a marriage," or "We had a difficult time with intimacy"? Did you have any idea what they were referring to?

Lisa and Brian

When Lisa and Brian got married, they knew they were supposed to be "intimate," but they really didn't know what that meant. Did that only mean sex? Could it also mean just hanging out watching TV partially dressed and enjoying the physical closeness of each other? Could it mean Brian brushing his teeth in the bathroom while Lisa is also in the bathroom taking a shower? When they were brave enough to ask a few trusted people, all they got were vague answers and advice as to what *not* to do but nothing concrete as to what *to* do. It took them several years of muddling through some hurts, disappointments, and confusion to finally realize that intimacy included all of the above mentioned and even more! When Brian and Lisa came to understand that real intimacy included fantastic sexual experiences as well as moments of just a little fondling or looking at each other in the "knowing" way, they both felt better about where they were as a couple and individuals. They had gained needed perspective—the view from eighteen thousand feet—and wished they had understood it sooner.

Think about times you have felt like you were being intimate with your spouse. Were you holding hands walking down the street? Were you playfully "copping a feel" as you passed one another in the hall? Were you having a meaningful discussion in bed with legs intertwined and maybe with some light touching going on? Was it a meaningful conversation where vulnerable emotions were involved and there was a mutual sense of understanding? Or were you having a great moment sexually? If you find yourself defining intimacy in terms of hand-holding, light touching, or playful kissing, you may want to ask your partner if that is how he or she would describe being intimate with you. Establishing a working definition of the word can do wonders for the next time your partner says, "I'd like to be intimate more often." You need to know if your partner is referring to something overtly sexual or hand-holding and cuddling.

Creating an atmosphere of intimacy between you and your partner is what will help to bring lasting commitment, satisfaction, and happiness. Many of us harbor fears that hold us back from truly establishing intimacy in our relationships. These fears can stem from the way we were raised, from trauma we may have experienced, misinformation, and distorted portrayals in the media.

Liz and Jason

Even after several years of marriage, Liz was truly uncomfortable being naked in front of Jason because she felt she was being immodest. Her good parents had taught her the importance of modesty from an early age but had neglected to talk with her about the difference between being modest for the world versus her future husband. Liz would uncover herself long enough to have sex with Jason, but then quickly cover up again. This made things difficult for Jason, who wanted to visually enjoy Liz's body and have her enjoy his. The tension this caused between them stopped their progression. Things began to change when Jason accidentally walked in on Liz getting dressed. She quickly covered up, but when she saw how much Jason was enjoying looking at her, she tried to work through her fear and allow him to just look and actually see her. After several uncomfortable moments, Liz calmed down and just stood there. Jason, trying to lighten things up, quickly took his clothes off so they would both be uncomfortable together. They ended up laughing, wrestling around, and, for the first time, just enjoying one another. The barrier was broken, and their feeling of intimacy greatly increased after that.

Four Corners of Intimacy or the Landscape of Intimacy

Our brains are designed to put things into categories. We don't like things that don't conform to some sort of definition or box. For example, the person you passed on the street this morning was broken down by your brain into height, hair color, type of clothing, gender, smell, and so on. Our brains also like to break down concepts into neat, little working definitions—clearly separated from each other. It's easy to classify intimacy into four areas: physical, emotional, sexual, and spiritual. We like to think of those four words as the foundation of a pyramid, with each corner contributing and eventually leading to the pinnacle of the pyramid where they join together. And while it's good to break it down into these terms, let's not forget the perspective we are looking for by getting completely bogged down with categories. The view from the top of the pyramid is much grander than the view from one of the corners of the base. Let's remember that we are trying to blend these concepts into one whole that will then create the type of intimacy we are longing for.

Another way of describing this concept would be a mountain landscape. When you see beautiful mountains standing majestically against the backdrop of the blue sky, what do you really see? Do you only see one peak or just the trees growing on top? No. You see the range as a whole, complete with trees, jagged peaks, canyons, cliffs, and wildlife. All these things combine to make the beautiful picture before you. This is the true nature of things, ideas, and concepts. Everything is interconnected and links with other things to make the whole. The idea of intimacy is no different. All four concepts need to be present—functioning and blending with each other—in order to create the whole.

Take a moment to step back from your relationship to see the whole picture of your intimacy. Is it a beautiful landscape or balanced pyramid, or is an entire aspect missing? Can you imagine what the mountains would look like without vegetation or if an entire section of hillside were simply missing? It would seem incomplete. Or if the pyramid were missing an entire side, it simply wouldn't stand. It's simple physics. Is there a part of your intimacy that is severely lacking? Let's spend a few moments discussing each of the four aspects of intimacy, keeping in mind the goal is to coalesce them in the end.

Trust, Safety, and Vulnerability

Three things have to be present in order to even begin building our intimacy pyramid—trust, safety, and vulnerability. First, trust means you need to be able to trust your partner and yourself to make good decisions regarding the relationship. Promises need to be kept. Second, it's almost impossible to have any sort of intimate connection with someone if you don't feel safe. If you find you are overly critical, abusive in any way, manipulative, and so on, you will jeopardize any ability for your partner to truly be intimate with you. Obviously, if you are experiencing any of the aforementioned things, all attempts at being intimate will be experienced as something negative and unwanted. Third, as with any building project, there are moments when things may seem uncertain, risky, or challenging. It's often in these moments we discover creative ways to solve problems, and we learn a lot about ourselves, our partners, and our relationship. Be open to these moments. Vulnerability creates space for creativity, growth, and new levels of trust and comfort.

Emotional Intimacy

Emotional intimacy can happen with or without sexual, physical, or spiritual intimacy and often has the components of trust, safety, and vulnerability. It's when our whole authentic selves are present—our strengths, our weaknesses, the moments worth celebrating, and the moments where we need a good cry or someone to vent to. It can be when your hair is undone, you are without makeup, and you are wearing sweatpants while having a delicious cup of conversation about life. It can be in the silence of a car ride, simply enjoying your partner's company. The hope is to create a space for acceptance, respect, and mutual understanding. Emotional intimacy is the meat of any relationship and will ultimately be what propels a relationship forward and fosters growth. It can foster sexual intimacy as well because there is already a sense of connection and trust, which in turn creates a sense of safety for times when we are the most vulnerable and open.

Diana and Brent

Diana loves talking with her friends and family and especially enjoys a great conversation with her girlfriends. She feels connected to them and they to her. However, Diana always comes home looking forward to "debriefing" with her husband. He usually jokes with her a little bit about how she still has several thousand words to get out of her system, while his word quota was used up hours ago. But he still listens and even asks a few questions. It's in times like these that Diana feels especially close to Brent because she feels safe. She trusts him with her thoughts and feelings and is able to be vulnerable enough to joke back with him about just how many words she has left to say. What Brent has come to understand about Diana is that when she feels emotionally connected to him in this way, it usually leads to her being open to physical intimacy later on. These seemingly mundane conversations are just what Diana needs to maintain her emotional intimacy with Brent, which then enhances other areas of the intimacy pyramid.

Sexual Intimacy & Physical Intimacy

Most of us think of sexual intimacy as just that—intimacy when we are having sex! However, zoologist Desmond Morris identified the following as progressions within sexual intimacy.

Eye to body
Eye to eye
Voice to voice
Hand to hand
Arm to shoulder
Arm to waist
Mouth to mouth
Hand to head
Hand to body
Mouth to breast
Hand to genitals
Genitals to genitals

Did you ever think that holding your spouse's hand was a form of sexual intimacy? Or looking into each other's eyes during a conversation? How about the way he or she plays with your hair as you're driving in your car? Sexual intimacy is far beyond what happens in the bedroom! Broadening your definition and understanding can open you and your relationship to wonderful possibilities. Physical and sexual intimacy can be as simple or elaborate as you want. Physical intimacy can be experienced in a variety of relationships such as with your friends, family, and children, whereas sexual intimacy is reserved for only your spouse. Where the touching occurs depends on your relationship and the appropriate touch for that relationship. Physical intimacy should lead to sexual intimacy with your spouse only.

Here are some scenarios to help you think about all the ways we experience physical and sexual intimacy and how physical touch doesn't necessarily mean physical or sexual intimacy. Think about the last time you saw your mother or a friend after a prolonged absence. You may have greeted them with a smile while gazing into their eyes, then given them a big, heartfelt hug. Now take that same scene and inject your favorite elementary school teacher. Do those scenarios feel different? What's the component that changes them for you? Now imagine you are at your favorite salon getting a pedicure or manicure. No matter the gender of the workers, you are relaxing as they rub your feet, exfoliate your legs, smooth lotion on, and paint your toes. Now take this same foot-rubbing scenario and replace the them with your spouse. Imagine you are at home, sitting on your comfortable couch, snuggling under a blanket. Does that change it for you? Does it feel more intimate? Do you feel more comfortable?

It's our relationship and connection that change physical and sexual touch to physical and sexual intimacy. Keep in mind that a sexual experience without some sort of emotional component is not necessarily intimate but is simply physical touch with a sexual component. Dr. Earl Henslin in his book, *This is Your Brain in Love*, said, "Sex for sex's sake, however, or sex with yourself or a stranger, does not produce the healthy high that sex-with-committed-love-in-marriage produces. It's 'scratching an itch' but without the component of a sacred committed relationship; sex never deeply satisfies your soul." If you find yourself only giving or receiving physical and sexual intimacy when your bodies or genitals are touching, you have a whole world of touch to explore!

Spiritual Intimacy

This area seems to be the least developed and the least understood. Many couples assume that just because they are both religious, spiritual intimacy will just naturally occur as they go about their daily or weekly church duties. However, some people have remarked that it's easier for them to have actual intercourse with their spouse than to kiss them because kissing is too intimate and they just don't have that kind of relationship. Many people find this sort of situation occurring with their level of spiritual intimacy. It's one thing to pray over the food at dinner, but it is another thing entirely to pray together at night, sharing worries, hopes, concerns, or fears.

Spiritual intimacy *is* the component that connects us as a couple to our Heavenly Father. It's being willing to share in one another's spiritual journeys. It's having a level of spiritual transparency and inviting our spouses into our areas of weakness as well strengths so that we can build and grow together.

Christine and Mark

Christine and Mark, although active in their ward, struggle in this area. Christine is afraid of sharing her innermost spiritual thoughts with Mark for fear he will laugh at her or just think she is weird. And while she has a difficult time sharing anything with Mark other than the "standard church answers," during any conversations concerning religion, God, or general spirituality, she will stand and share her most sacred feelings during her Relief Society meeting. She's just not sure she trusts Mark enough to open this side of herself to him. Instead, she and Mark go through the motions of everything they're "supposed" to be doing without making any sort of meaningful spiritual connection with each other. Christine feels bad about hiding this part of herself from Mark, but she is unsure about how to move through it.

After giving it some thought, Christine decided her spiritual side was a part of her worth sharing and felt like doing so would increase the feeling of intimacy between her and Mark. However, she was still somewhat afraid of what his reaction might be so she decided to begin her conversation with Mark by telling him she had something important to share and that she would appreciate him just listening without laughing or making any "weird faces." Mark was happy to oblige— especially since he knew exactly what she was expecting from him.

The "Ideal" Intimacy Pyramid versus the "Real" Intimacy Pyramid

Building a pyramid is slow and tedious work. It will not happen overnight, over a year, or over a decade. Once you are committed to the process you can begin, brick by brick, establishing your relationship pyramid. However, you may find one side much larger than the other one year and another side much larger than that the next year or even day! You may even have to tear down entire sides and start over again! All of that is okay. This is your relationship and your intimacy. The fact that you are in this project together is sometimes all you'll have, but it's still enough. Over time, and with work, patience, love, fun, and forgiveness, you will see your mountain landscape or pyramid beginning to take shape. Revel in it because it is yours—your creation— together. It is unique, special, and a wonder to behold.

THE NUTS AND BOLTS

"Intimacy" is difficult to define. Are we talking emotional, physical, spiritual, or mental intimacy? What does it mean? Although we desire to be intimate and have intimate relationships, we struggle with understanding the key components of intimacy. In this first chapter, we present two analogies to help break down this idea: the four corners of a pyramid and a mountain landscape.

A pyramid has a base with four distinct corners that eventually converge. Intimacy too has its foundation in the emotional, physical, mental, and spiritual, with the hope that the four corners will grow together and converge, creating a feeling of complete "oneness." Each couple or individual may struggle with one or more of those areas, making the pyramid somewhat unsteady or imbalanced. This chapter encourages you to think about those four areas and evaluate your relationship based on those concepts. Take a moment to reflect on whether one side of the pyramid is high and completely dominating the others. What does that do to promote or hinder your relationship with your spouse? Are you willing to spend some time shoring up the other sides in order to make a balanced pyramid? The other analogy involves a mountain landscape. If you gaze at any mountain range, you will notice the mountains, of course, as well as the plants, trees, barren areas, and perhaps animals. There are many aspects to a mountain range that, together, make the whole thing beautiful. If we ignore any of the aspects, the picture is incomplete and less enjoyable. No two mountain ranges are exactly alike, just as your relationship and the intimacy that occurs within it are also unique. Each relationship has crags, rocky cliffs, beautiful meadows, high peaks, and low valleys that contribute to the overall beauty, majesty, and unique nature of it. Try not to compare your relationship with anyone else's but focus on what is good and unique about yours. Also, by simply noticing your relationship, you may see areas that could use some extra attention—whether in the emotional, physical, spiritual, or mental areas. This book will help you discover those areas and give you the tools you need to achieve the relationship you desire.

Chapter Questions for Real-Life Application

To further solidify what you've just read, as well as to help you think more deeply on this subject, here are a few questions to think about:

1. How do you define intimacy?

2. How does your partner define intimacy? Are your definitions similar?

3. Discuss with your partner or think about a time when you felt physically intimate in a non-sexual setting.

4. Draw a picture of your "intimacy pyramid" and label the sides. Does it look how you expected? What does your partner's look like? Which areas could use some extra attention?

5. Are there times when you don't feel safe with your partner? How does that affect your ability to be and feel intimate with your partner? Is this something you can discuss with your partner?

2
THE GODLY DESIGN OF INTIMACY
Yes, intimacy is part of His design

IT IS DIFFICULT TO DESCRIBE GOD WITHOUT USING METAPHOR AND analogy. Let's use the mountain range analogy again for a few moments. When most people are asked to draw a mountain, they draw a simple triangle shape without much form. That's the human idea of mountains. God's idea is much different. There are incredible peaks, valleys, crags, cliffs, vegetation, and animal life. Some of the tallest mountain ranges are covered by ocean waters miles deep, while others have been worn down with age, experience, brutal storms, and acts of nature. God invites us to be intimate with Him through His natural creations and teaches us that all things, including us and our relationships, are unique depending on our circumstances and placement on the earth. He invites us to feel His fierceness and wildness as we're climbing jagged paths. He invites us to feel His tenderness when we pick a flower and brush it gently across our face. He even allows us to criticize and mock His creations if we so choose. He seems to be with us in all of our developmental stages and is pleased when we choose to grow, to enlarge our vision, and to learn to treat His children and creations the same way in which He interacts with us. He is completely open to us and desires intimacy with us through His creations.

We too are His creations and have been given the ability to choose to be intimate with each other as well as Him. The landscapes of our lives shape our patterns of intimacy as well. We don't fit into neat little triangle-shaped mountains as we sometimes wish we would. We can be fierce and wild, tender and soft, worn-down or invigorated. However, in order for this discussion to have some concreteness, we must put a few things into categories. It seems there are three universal parts to a mountain range as well: the mountains themselves, the vegetation or life living on them, and erosion, which serves to shape and give them unique qualities.

In Genesis we read, "And God saw everything that he had made, and, behold it was very good. And the evening and the morning were the sixth day." Notice this scripture comes toward the end of the creative periods and not at the beginning. By this time man (and woman) had been created, which means God was calling all His creations, including us, "good." After all, according to the bumper sticker, "God don't make no junk!"

If we truly take that scripture literally, it has to follow that everything about our bodies would be included in that statement. In fact, we know that our bodies are one of the two gifts—the other being the ability to make choices—that God has bestowed upon us while we are on this earth. Our bodies are essential to His plan to bring His spirit children to earth, giving us the opportunity to experience all that having a mortal body could be. We also know that "men are that they might have joy" (2 Nephi 2:25). The word "joy" implies much more than just living out some meager existence until we die. It means that God actually desires we be happy while here on earth as well! That being said, let's look at how our bodies have been designed to actually confirm his statement that they are good.

Shannon and Clark

Shannon and Clark sought counseling soon after they were married. Shannon was having a difficult time wanting to be intimate with Clark at all. When asked about it, Shannon remarked that she "just wasn't ready to have kids yet." The counselor asked Shannon to explain what she meant by that statement. Shannon revealed that she was brought up to believe her body was designed only for "making babies," and therefore she and Clark should only have sex when they were going to actually try to have a child. Shannon went on to say how attracted she was to Clark and that she was excited at the prospect of actually having sex with him, but that she just wasn't ready for a child.

While Shannon is exactly right in her belief that sexual intercourse does have the potential to create life and therefore must be treated as sacred and something not to be trifled with, Shannon was missing the other half of the equation—she hadn't fully understood the full design her body was created for. She was missing out on some of that "joy" God said could be found on earth.

So how do we resolve the fact that God created our bodies—every aspect of them—and called them "good" and then hoped we would find "joy" while here on earth? Sex was not an accident. Sex was not an afterthought. Sex was not deemed unworthy or forbidden. On the other hand, sex has such incredible potential and power to deeply unite a couple *and* create life, that we have been given very strict commandments that sex only be used within the confines of a legal and lawful marriage.

For women especially, sex as a purely pleasurable experience can be a difficult concept. After all, our model for female sexual purity is Mary, the mother of Jesus. While most people accept that she had other children besides Jesus, she is more commonly referenced as a "virgin" and put on a pedestal as such. We teach our young girls to be pure and virtuous, which they should be, but we don't discuss with them how they can be pure and virtuous within the confines of an intimate marital relationship. Their virtue doesn't change—it becomes enhanced with the added ability to create life as well as bring "life" to the relationship with their husband. Mary was undoubtedly intimate with her husband Joseph. She had all the same impulses and desires other women do. Our society keeps her so "clean" and set apart from the earthiness of reality, it can be a challenge to use her as a model of female sexuality.

If you don't know what the clitoris is, which Shannon did not and Clark had heard of vaguely, please be sure to read the chapter entitled "Sex Ed 101." Although there were other issues Shannon and Clark had to work out, they both gained a wonderful, new perspective on human sexuality after opening up to the idea that procreation did not have to be the only reason to have sex. Shannon was reminded that God—not Satan—created our bodies and their functions and uses, and that the clitoris has no other function than that of bringing sexual pleasure to a woman (you will still need to read chapter three in order to fully understand this concept). She then realized that God didn't make a mistake in his creation of her. Shannon and Clark began to see their relationship as unique. As they included God in the "creation" of their relationship, a beautiful landscape began to take shape.

The Bible compares our bodies to a temple. A temple is a place where one can commune with God and learn deep doctrine about who we are, who He is, where we came from, and where we are going. Along with that, we learn the process of stages of learning and development that bring us ultimately into His presence, so we may someday partake of life with Him. It is a place where we can leave the cares of the world behind and truly commune with God or seek intimacy with God and His son without any pretense or worry. We generally leave our temple experience feeling renewed, rejuvenated, and refreshed. There is a sense of closeness with God, and we look forward to the next time we can feel that same closeness with Him. How can we bring this experience into our relationships with each other? No pretense, nothing feigned, nothing deceptive or trying to make it look like this or that. We come to Him real, flawed, unsure, vulnerable, and willing to submit ourselves to Him and learn what He desires to teach us.

Take This Idea into a Marriage

Let's put all this into the concept of physical intimacy within a marriage. This unique relationship, which is not shared between neighbors, general acquaintances, or relatives, is only shared between husband and wife. It is through this vulnerable sexual experience that a man and woman come together with openness and trust. Together they create something new—not just a child, but a new entity that no one else can replicate. It is just between them, unique and personal. They are "creating" this unique oneness, between themselves, before God. The individual man and woman become a "they" in that moment, and the lines between them become blurred. Together they are more than they are separately and have a spiritual synergy. This process enhances them yet also has the power to destroy them. It has the power to create and the power to dissolve. Remember, all things have both powers inherent within them—good and evil, light and darkness, pleasure and pain. This vulnerability is the only way that life can and will be created. Without vulnerability, the creative process is destroyed by control, and choice is taken away. When there is no choice, the creative process is destroyed and pain, anger, resentment, and blame rule and dissolve intimacy.

Physical intimacy with a spouse has the potential to leave us feeling as we did upon leaving the temple or other spiritual experiences. We experience the same feelings of refreshment and rejuvenation, and our relationship renewed. You may experience a new or deeper sense of unity between you and your spouse, and, ideally, there is a joyful antic-ipation of the next time you can be together in such a close, intimate way.

Of course, we don't have a miraculous spiritual experience every time we attend the temple. We sometimes accidentally fall asleep or let our minds wander into other areas of our lives. Does this mean we are worshiping inappropriately or that we have not learned how to best achieve perfect temple worship? Of course not. It means we are tired, spent, and overwhelmed. It also suggests that all of these emotions and experiences can happen and are acceptable before God as part of "real" relationships.

It is likewise unreasonable to expect there will be bells and whistles every time we are sexually intimate with our spouse. If you're feeling like you're supposed to be having some sort of rich spiritual experience each time you are intimate with your spouse, please consider just how often you are having that type of experience at church or at the temple. We all know that there is "opposition in all things," but we forget that this concept applies to *all* things, including our spiritual and sexual experiences. If we never had lulls in our spiritual experiences, how would we know when we were even having them? The same goes for our sexual experiences with our spouse. We need to have a variety of experiences with our spouse in order to appreciate those times when we truly do feel renewed, rejuvenated, refreshed, and at one with each other.

The flora and fauna covering the mountain landscapes around us are incredibly varied and interesting. Some aspects are dangerous and difficult, while other aspects are inviting and restful. All the life found within the mountains makes up their beauty and depth. These same aspects give color, depth, and meaning to our intimate relationship with our spouse as well as with God.

In Gary Thomas's book, *Sacred Marriage*, he reminds us of the ancient Israelites' perspective on sex. The Hebrews had a wonderful idea of how physical intimacy between a man and a woman could be likened to the kind of intimacy we hope to experience with God. Of course the Hebrews were concerned about procreation for the sake of procreation because continuing the family line, or the "chosen people," was one of the most fundamental principles of the time. However, there was an understanding that sex was to be experienced outside of the realm of procreation as well. The women of ancient Israel were granted three "fundamental rights": food, clothing, and the "onah"—which means physical intimacy beyond that of just procreation (205–206).

There is an ancient Hebrew text entitled "The Holy Letter" (written by Nahmanides in the thirteenth century). It describes sex as a mystical experience of meeting with God: "Through the act (of intercourse) they become partners with God in the act of creation. This is the mystery of what the sages said, 'When a man unites with his wife in holiness, the Shekinah is between them in the mystery of man and woman'"(60). Thomas goes on to say, "The breadth of this statement is sobering when you consider that this shekinah glory is the same presence experienced by Moses when God met with him face-to-face." (See Exodus 24:15–18.) This sacred embrace or what is called in scripture as wrestling with God and angels was seen as the highest order of spiritual enlightenment—to know Him and He to know you. We are not intimating that this was a sexual encounter, but a new closeness was achieved between God and man. (See Genesis 32.)

What does that tell us about the kind of intimacy God would like His children to experience as spouses as well as the kind of intimacy He desires with us individually and as a couple? If this is a difficult concept for you, consider the idea that Gary Thomas put forth in his book. Consider gratitude. We are counseled by our leaders and by the scriptures to be grateful in all things. Have you considered expressing gratitude for your sexuality and sexual desires? Have you felt grateful you are attracted to your spouse or she to you? While we may express gratitude for our health or other things pertaining to our bodies, perhaps we can also express gratitude to God for being able to experience the pure joy and pleasure that can come through healthy sexual experiences. This could help you begin to see the reality of sex, for the sake of sex, as an eternal concept. It's easy to believe in a God who allows us to draw near to Him during times of pain, such as fasting when we may be experiencing difficulties. It's more difficult to believe in a God who also wants us to draw near to Him during times of happiness or pure pleasure. But He wants us to be as happy and fulfilled as we can be while here on earth, which is one reason He created sexual intimacy.

Let's return to the mountain range analogy. Sex is many things. It can be used to strengthen and solidify our relationship, like the mountains themselves. It can be beautiful, joyful, playful, wild, and wistful, like the flora and fauna found on the mountains. It is unique and sometimes sacred. It can also be painful—especially if there have been unpleasant learning moments within the relationship. But it is this uniqueness—like the erosion that creates the breathtaking shapes, cliffs, and caverns—that creates depth and breadth and scope. All these experiences create the beautiful landscape that is your intimate relationship with your spouse and God.

God makes covenants with us to love each other as He loves us. Let's recall from our experience with the Father and the Son just how they love us; how Christ has suffered for all of our pains, grief, and illnesses; how He intimately knows our sorrows, heartaches, triumphs, and joys. How many of us can compare our effort and energy to the Lord's energy and effort He expends for us? Do we put forth the same kind of effort He does when it concerns our spouses? Have we strived with all that is in us to understand as He strives to understand us? Do we feel after them as completely as we expect Him to feel after us or consider others as He considers us? He loves us even in our weakness, sin, anger, foolishness, pity, and shame. He even loves us in our pride and boastfulness and reaches after us when we run from Him or when we forsake His ways. We often want to be understood before we understand and consoled before we are willing to console. We want to be loved before we learn what it is like to really love and to have our prayers answered before we are willing to do all we can do to satisfy the longings and desires of those with whom we live, and those who love us.

As we love, serve, care, listen, encourage, comfort, and know, so shall we be loved, served, cared for, listened to, encouraged, comforted, and known. Intimacy is a two-way street. We take away from it only as much as we have contributed to it. It serves us only as we serve it. We too often ask far more of intimacy than what we are willing to give to intimacy. For this reason so much of the world's population is desperately turning to the biggest counterfeit known to humans— pornography. It is Lucifer's well-planned, well-oiled machine to lead us away from real intimacy and real love. Pornography is his false substitute for the work required to truly be intimate with the Father and the Son. Only as we wrestle with Him for this gracious gift of closeness, of understanding, of sacrifice, are we allowed to be shown how to share real intimacy with our spouses.

To create anything, we need to get our self out of the way. We share who and what we really are and then we remove ourselves from the need to control the situation. The more we attempt to control, the less intimacy we receive. Think of the creation process of conceiving and giving birth. The man comes to the women and desires to have a relationship, knowing that a child may be conceived through this close, intimate contact and lovemaking. He can only enter her by, through, and with her permission and mutual desire. If not, it is not love that is being made but control; then only hate, fear, resentment, and sorrow can be produced from this false, forced sexuality. With her permission and sanction, he is allowed to leave part of himself with her. He cannot choose which sperm may impregnate her or which egg will be fertilized. He must allow this healthy serendipity to function and get himself out of the way so life can be created and allowed.

The more we try to control this process, the more complications occur. Creation requires chance and room to expand. Serendipity is that space. It's where creativity, hope, and love flourish and grow. Randomness is also an important aspect of this relationship. Again, no two mountain landscapes are the same. While there is an inherent similar structure, each range has developed differently according to time and the elements surrounding it. Being human, we try so hard to overcontrol our lovemaking and intimacy. Instead of allowing for creative space to allow our intimacy to flourish, we create comparatives, standards, and patterns and procedures that get old and tired in our relationships. Pretty soon we end up with task-oriented, job-structured sex that is no longer creative, loving, nurturing, or fun.

God wants us to live like He lives—not become robotic in nature and stuck in ruts that torment and try us. Notice how intimate He is with us in nature. Think about when you have walked on the beach, feeling the sand between your toes, listening to the crash of the waves, breathing in the salt air, feeling the sun on your skin, and seeing the entire beautiful landscape. That is God being intimate with you, in a physical way. All your senses are involved. Your body is feeling God, breathing God, seeing God, hearing God, and sensing God—literally taking Him into ourselves in a physical way. That type of intimacy generally only happens with one other person—our spouse. God wants to be close to us—not in a sexual way—but in an intimate and creative way. He wants us to experience what He experiences and desires to share with us in that experience.

THE NUTS AND BOLTS

In Genesis we read, "And God saw everything that he had made, and, behold it was very good. And the evening and the morning were the sixth day." Notice this scripture comes toward the end of the creative periods and not at the beginning. Man (and woman) had been created by this time, which means God was calling all His creations, including us, "good." This would include our sexuality, which had also been created as part of our physical body.

Our bodies are one of our greatest gifts given to us from God. We shouted for joy at the prospect of even being able to receive one! When a baby is born, we spend a lot of time kissing its face, neck, ears, and so on. Studies have shown that babies do not thrive without physical touch. This phenomenon doesn't end with babies. As we grow, we need and depend upon physical touch and experiences.

There is nothing shameful, wrong, or dirty about simply enjoying the feel of someone kissing your face, hands, neck, and so on. It is lovely to experience the rush we get when we gaze upon the people we love. When we hear the sounds of our spouse walking through the house or singing in the shower, we feel a sense of contentment.

Our loving Heavenly Father, who desires to share all He has with us, has created our bodies in His image. These bodies were designed for physical experiences—and lots of them. If we are like He is, then we could logically suppose that Heavenly Father also enjoys physical experiences with His body as well. It's all part of the plan.

Let's return to the mountain-range analogy. Sex is many things. It can be used to strengthen and solidify our relationship, like the mountains themselves. It can be beautiful, joyful, playful, wild, and wistful, like the flora and fauna found on the mountains. It is unique and sometimes sacred. It can also be painful—especially if there have been painful learning moments within the relationship. But it is this uniqueness, like the erosion that occurs throughout mountain landscapes—causing breathtaking shapes, cliffs, and caverns—that creates depth and breadth and scope. These experiences create the beautiful landscape of your intimate relationship with your spouse and God.

God wants us to live like He lives, not become robotic and stuck in ruts that torment and try us. For example, notice how intimate He is with us in nature. Think about when you have walked on the beach, feeling the sand between your toes, listening to the crash of the waves, breathing in the salt air, feeling the sun on your skin, and seeing the beautiful landscape. That is God being intimate with you, in a physical way. All your senses are involved. Your body is feeling God, breathing God, seeing God, hearing God, and sensing God—literally taking Him into ourselves in a physical way. That type of intimacy generally only happens with one other person—our spouse. God wants to be close to us—not in a sexual way—but in an intimate and creative way. He wants us to experience what He experiences and desires to share with us in that experience.

Chapter Questions for Real-Life Application

1. What have you been taught about God and intimacy? Do you feel

like anything you have learned interferes or adds to your relationship with your spouse?

2. Go to your scriptures and see if you can find references dealing with intimacy. Share with your spouse what you found and discuss why that reference felt like intimacy to you.

3. Take a walk, touch a tree, breathe in the air, notice the beauty, feel the sunlight, and enjoy the moonlight without any technology. Allow yourself to feel the presence of Heavenly Father in an intimate way.

3
SEX ED 101
How our bodies work

"I REMEMBER (RECALLS MARK) WALKING THROUGH THE AISLE AT the bookstore where the 'sex books' were and trying to look at the covers without anyone noticing. I just wanted more information about the whole subject but was too embarrassed to actually pick up a book about it!"

Here's the part of the book where we are going to get real and find some clarity and understanding about how our bodies work. It's easy to get hung up on the sexual side of our bodies and lose sight of their human functionality. Though our genitals are our pleasure centers, they also serve basic human needs. In case your parents neglected to inform you, and you missed your one day of high school biology when the subject was addressed, here is some basic but incredibly helpful information to give you a much better grasp of your own body as well as your partner. Since there are some great books and resources out there on human anatomy, we are not going to go into great depth, but we will give you the most relevant information as it relates to sexual intimacy.

The little girl in the movie *Kindergarten Cop* says it very matter-of-factly when she says, "Boys have a penis and girls have a vagina." True, but fortunately and unfortunately it's not as simple as simply having one of these organs. Let's break it down a bit more so we understand what everything else is and what it does, starting with what took place while we were still in the womb regarding our sexuality. After all, the brain, and not the penis or vagina, is the largest sex organ if you really stop to think about it!

Sexual Organ Development

The process of becoming sexual begins in the womb and continues throughout your life cycle. In fact, it doesn't stop until you are safely dead. That's right, even when you are ninety-five, you are still developing as a sexual being. You've never experienced age-fifty-seven sex until you are fifty-seven, and so on! This all started of course in the beginning, when you were just the successful combining of a sperm from your dad and an egg from your mom.

At the time of your conception, when the combination of your genetic materials from both your parents led to the first physical differences between you becoming a little girl or boy, both bodies looked female. For, female is Mother Nature's recipe. In other words, all of us would be little girls if the H-Y antigen, a substance which is controlled by the Y chromosome, didn't start to transform little female gonads and bodies into little male testes and boy bodies. This hormone wash takes place approximately seven weeks into gestation. In other words, while in the womb, all little boys started out as little girls. The process of actually becoming male is a three-fold undertaking: First, the hormone washing differentiates the internal sexual structures in our bodies. Second, it starts the development of the external sexual organs, making boy parts out of the girl parts: testes are formed from ovaries; penile glands, or the head of the penis, are formed from clitoral glands; and penile shafts or the shaft of the penis are formed from the clitoral shaft and the labia minora (the labia minora are the folds found in women on the outer and inner lips of the woman's genitalia at the opening which leads to the vagina). The scrotum is formed from the labia majora. In everyday language, all of the man's genitalia are externalized from the woman's internal and external parts, and they are used to form the internal and external sexual organs of the developing male.

Third—and this is a really big point—this process of the H-Y antigen washes over the brain and causes that girl brain to become a testosterone-washed boy brain, ready to do all the cultural, societal, and behavioral male-oriented and socially related structures imposed upon it as an adult male brain.

Why is this important? The more you know about your own genitals and your partner's, the better! You are more likely to have successful interactions with these parts and avoid the often-damaging myths we rely on in sexual relationships.

Okay, now that we understand how we developed our physiological organs, let's take a closer look at the structure of each gender. This part may be a little dry but well worth the time to make sure you truly know what you mean when you make sexually related statements. For example, if you say you would like your "vagina" touched, is that accurate or could you mean something else?

Here's a quick story about "Kermit" and "Miss Piggy" to help illustrate why you truly want to be able to use and understand all these terms.

It's interesting that we learn from an early age many slang words for sexual parts that often are more accepted and comfortable than correct terminology. A well-educated married couple came in for sexual counseling and marital issues. The man and woman always talked in the third-person about their own sexual anatomy. This couple used two of the characters from The Muppets as names for their own sexual parts. The husband would address his wife's genitals as "Miss Piggy," and he would call his "Kermit." They would use their own given first names when communicating on any topic other than sex. When sex was the topic, they would refer to their sexual organs as Miss Piggy and Kermit. So the conversation would go something like this:

"Kermit would really like to connect with Miss Piggy tonight. Could you ask Miss Piggy if she might be interested?"

This created for them a buffer in any sexual conflict, for it was "Miss Piggy and Kermit"—not they—who were having a hard time with the sexual interactions. She would say:

"Miss Piggy didn't like that sexual interaction so much and wished Kermit would be more gentle and have more patience with Miss Piggy in getting ready for sex. Kermit is just always in such a hurry, and Miss Piggy wants him to participate more in foreplay before taking care of his need when Miss Piggy is not ready. Tell Kermit if he doesn't slow down, he is going to miss the train next time, and Miss Piggy will leave the station without him."

Kermit would feel bad and even send Miss Piggy flowers to make up for the sexual displeasure or concern, with the husband not even owning up to the fact that he was even involved in the process. Neither took personal responsibility for his or her own involvement, actions, or behaviors regarding their sexual experience.

This is why we will discuss correct terminology and functions of male and female sexual organs—so all of us can appropriately label, talk about, and identify our own genitals and those of our partners.

REAL RELATIONSHIP TIP!
Sex Education and Kids

Many people express the concern that by discussing sex, it sanctions premarital sex. However, the opposite is true. By teaching our children about sex in the safety of our home, we have the opportunity to choose what we teach and give guidance and educate from a gospel perspective. If we leave sexual education to their peers, society, or the media, they may receive inaccurate and unhealthy information that can make them more curious. "The Family: A Proclamation to the World" states, "Husband and wife have a solemn responsibility to love and care for each other and for their children. 'Children are an heritage of the Lord' (Psalm 127:3). Parents have a sacred duty to rear their children in love and righteousness, to provide for their physical and spiritual needs, and to teach them to love and serve one another, observe the commandments of God, and be law-abiding citizens wherever they live." We can't think of anything more important than helping our children feel happy and healthy in their God-given bodies by teaching them about all the miraculous things a body can do.

Male Anatomy and Terms

Penis: There are many components of the penis. It is used for intercourse, ejaculating semen, and to urinate. The penis itself has three sections that contribute to pleasure and sexuality:

1) The *glans* or the "head of the penis" has numerous nerve endings

due to a thin skin and is very sensitive to touch. In a circumcised penis, it is easy to differentiate the head because it is the helmet-looking object at the end of the penis. In an uncircumcised penis, the head is merely hiding "under the hood" and is exposed when the skin is pulled back.

2) The *frenulum* is a small piece of skin on the underside of the penis. It is where the shaft and the glans meet and can be a man's most sensitive spot.

3) The *shaft* is just below the glans and is what basically makes up the remainder of the penis. The shaft can become thicker and hard when aroused, allowing penetration and intercourse to occur.

Erection: This is when the penis is hard and typically "standing up." An erection occurs when there is increased blood flow. Though it may seem that men only have erections when they are aroused, they can occur spontaneously with or without sexual arousal and sometimes for no apparent reason. An erect penis is about 9.5 centimeters or 4 inches long. Size differences in penises usually occur in a flaccid or non-erect state.

Testes/Testicles: These are the male sex glands and are located behind the penis in the pouch of skin called the scrotum. They make and store sperm and are the main center for the male hormone, testosterone. The scrotum contracts involuntarily as a result of sexual stimulation or from exercise or temperature variance. In cold, the scrotum contracts closer to the body and in heat, hangs further away. Just think of the *Seinfeld* episode in which George is mortified due to the "shrinkage" he experienced from swimming in a cold pool!

The testes are male gonads paired within the scrotal sac. They are highly sensitive to pressure or touch. These organs produce the hormone testosterone that controls sexual development and is primarily responsible for sexual interest and function. The testes produce billions of sperm each year. When touched in a way that feels good to your partner, they add positive sensations to a sexual experience. Testicles are very sensitive, so touching or caressing with too much pressure or firmness can create tremendous discomfort.

Prostate Gland: The prostate gland is about the size of a walnut and is located directly below the bladder. The prostate produces clear liquid that makes up about 30 percent of the seminal fluid, or the liquid that is expelled from the penis during ejaculation. The other 70 percent of the fluid comes from the seminal vessels.

Perineum: This is the ridged skin between the testicles and the anus and buttocks. This is a very sexually sensitive spot on the male body and may be an area that is unfamiliar territory for most women and maybe some men. This would be a good opportunity to open up conversation with your husband and ask him if touching or caressing it feels good to him. See "common erogenous zones" to learn more about this sensitive spot.

Kara's Story

"My husband and I were out for the evening with our closest couple friends. We were always pretty open with our conversations, but this particular night the topic of sex came up. The girls were curious about how many erections men had in a typical day. The responses from the guys all varied, but I was shocked and baffled when the guys said that erections sometimes happened for no reason at all and were happening without sexual stimulation! I mean, I knew that my husband sometimes woke up with what he called a 'morning missile,' but I guess I hadn't really thought about how often those types of erections could occur."

Kara learned that a penis can spontaneously become hard because that is what it is designed to do. It can grow, shrink, or stay hard for long periods of time or lose its firmness after a short time. All of this can happen without any sexual stimulation, thought, or action.

Female Outer Anatomy

The female anatomy is a little bit more complex when compared to its male counterpart. Breasts must be included. Also, with the vagina there is internal and external anatomy that are sexually relevant. Let's start with the outer anatomy.

Breasts: In many societies, the breasts are seen as having a dual purpose as both a utility for breastfeeding and as a sexual object and sexual-stimulation facility. A special erotic allure that is directly related to sex and attractiveness is given to the breasts in the United States and other western cultures. There is absolutely no evidence to suggest that breast size has any relationship to a woman's sexual capacity, interest, or her desire and pleasure. Sexual excitement, from experiencing breast stimulation is no different in women with small or large breasts. In some cases, breast augmentation can lead to diminished sensation and stimulation. In the excitement phase of a women's sexual response cycle, the areola—the brownish area of the female breast—begins to swell. This swelling produces nipple erection.

Vulva: This word means "covering" and refers to the collective external genitalia, which are commonly but mistakenly referred to as the vagina. The genitalia include:

Mons: Mons comes from the Latin word, "mound." It's the area above the pubic bone that consists of a cushion of fatty tissue covered by skin and pubic hair. It is covered by many nerve endings that can provide great stimulation and pleasant feelings. In many women, this area can bring as much pleasure as direct or indirect clitoral contact.

Clitoris: By design, the clitoris serves only as a pleasure spot. It is a gift from our Creator who wants us to experience physical pleasure and joy. It is located just below the pubic bone and has a ball-like shape. It is much bigger than most people think. It is approximately 2–3 centimeters long and has a "hood" or covering similar to an uncircumcised penis. This area is highly sensitive and can be overstimulated with too much direct pressure. However, it is most often by stimulation of the clitoris that women are able to experience orgasm. About 80 percent of women will experience an orgasm this way rather than from sexual intercourse alone. During sex or arousal, the clitoris will double in size and become "erect" much like a penis. This is a great time to ask your wife how she likes to be touched. This varies from woman to woman and can change from moment to moment, due to the sensitive nature of the clitoris.

Labia: The outer lips of the labia are called the labia majora. These are skin folds that cover large amounts of fat tissue and thin layers of smooth muscle. Pubic hair grows on the sides of these outer lips. Many nerve endings are situated within them, which provides pleasure if gently stimulated. The labia also provide protection for the vaginal opening and the urethral urinary opening. The inner lips are the Labia minora. They contain small internal blood vessels and nerve endings. These inner lips meet with the clitoris, forming the clitoral hood. Both these labia can be a significant source of pleasure and sensation. These outer and inner lips vary in size and appearance from woman to woman.

Perineum: This is the skin that goes from the bottom of the vulva to the anus and is what typically tears during childbirth. While the perineum may not directly produce pleasure, it can be a pleasurable area with light touch.

Female Internal Genitalia

Vagina: Dr. Miriam Stoppard, M.D. describes the vagina in her book, *The Magic of Sex*: "The vagina is a potential rather than an actual space." The walls of the vagina are often touching unless something is inserted between them. It is not simply an open space. The vagina is usually no more than four inches in length, and like the penis, the vagina can expand and contract. The vaginal opening can tighten down to be the size of a pencil and expand to be large enough to deliver a baby! Thanks to the elasticity of the vagina, it can accommodate nearly every size of penis. If an erect penis enters the vagina before it is fully expanded, the vagina will quickly adjust to accommodate the penis.

Vaginal Walls: The vaginal walls release secretions that aid in lubrication for sex. Once arousal occurs, the secretions may look like balls of sweat. In addition to their sexual function, they also help in the "self-cleaning" function of the vagina. Other than good hygienic habits, women do not need to take additional measures to clean their vagina.

Hymen: The hymen is the piece of tissue that blocks all or some of the entrance to the vagina. Usually the hymen is broken through vigorous physical activity. During intercourse, if it is still intact, it may or may not break. If it does break, a woman may experience slight cramping and bleeding.

Cervix: The cervix is known as the "neck" of the uterus, connecting the vagina to the uterus. There is a small opening at the top of the uterus that allows for menstrual blood from the uterus to flow into the vagina. It is this same opening that dilates during labor and allows the baby to pass through the uterus and vagina.

G-spot: The "g-spot" must be mentioned because it is the most media-friendly spot within the female body. Magazines seem to love to help women and men find the g-spot. However, very few women have a clear idea of where their g-spot is or how to access it during sex and achieve orgasm from its stimulation. Though this spot may be a hot spot in terms of nerves and sensitivity, don't feel bad or pressure to achieve orgasm from your g-spot—you may or may not find it!

Women, if you are unfamiliar with your own anatomy, consider getting a book showing your anatomy and a mirror so you can understand your body.

Arousal and Orgasm

Both males and females go through an arousal cycle, but experiences are very different. You may find it takes a woman a bit longer to warm-up sexually. Additionally, a woman may not necessarily reach orgasm; a man can require little touch or time to achieve orgasm. A male orgasm typically leaves him feeling relaxed and sleepy. A female's orgasm may also produce sleepiness, or it may leave her feeling like she's ready to go out a run a race!

The great news about this is that there are physiological reasons behind these differences. Recognizing this can help you understand yourself and your partner and improve the intimate experience. Let's first start with what happens for men and women during the arousal cycle.

Male Arousal Cycle

Men generally experience four phases in their arousal cycle: First, men typically experience initial stimulation and excitement. Physiologically, this means his breath might quicken, his heart starts beating faster, and his penis may start to become hard or erect. As more blood starts to flow to his penis and it continues to increase in size, he hits the next phase. At the second phase, he reaches the plateau phase where his penis has reached maximum engorgement and is as hard as it will get. This is where heightened foreplay or intercourse is occurring and can be the most intense phase right before ejaculation. Some men describe this experience as feeling like they are going to explode—literally and figuratively. Keep in mind, it can also be a common experience for men to experience a hard erection and soft erection before returning to hard again during the plateau phase. The third phase is the climax, where he reaches orgasm and ejaculates. Simply stated, this is when the semen is pushed out of the body. This can be a whole-body experience including shortness of breath, tightening of the muscles, and pulsating of the penis. The testicles move up and into the body. Fourth is the resolution or recovery phase when his penis becomes soft and returns to its "everyday" state. It can take some time—or several hours—for a man to be able to achieve a new erection.

Female Arousal Cycle

Women will go through similar arousal stages but experience them differently: First, women typically don't experience immediate arousal like men but can be "turned on" by light touching, slow movement, and flat out patience from their partner as their bodies warm to the task. During the second phase, the vagina becomes lubricated, breast size increases (up to 25 percent), and the labia clitoris swells. The clitoris produces heightened pleasure, but be sure to check-in with your partner on the kind of touch she likes because it can also be increasingly sensitive and tender. Third phase, which may not always happen, is orgasm. Like your husband, you may feel like you are going to burst right before you orgasm. Keep in mind, 50–75 percent of women will never achieve orgasm through intercourse alone but require clitoral stimulation. Just like in men, a woman's climax will be a full-body experience, causing toes to curl and breath to tighten. Additionally, women can experience multiple orgasms. Fourth is the recovery phase where the heart rate starts to slow down and the body begins to relax. The labia and clitoris will begin to diminish in size and the body will return to its normal state.

Barring a physiological problem, most people have the potential to successfully move through the four stages of sexual arousal. However, the process can be short-circuited for various reasons including lack of trust in a partner, anxiety, and other factors. According to Melinda Wenner's research, individuals have to let go of all fear and anxiety in order to achieve orgasm. If you find this is how you feel, review the sexual history or sexual complications chapters.

Where to Go from Here

Phew! That was a lot of information to get through, but it was extremely important. You wouldn't get in a car and expect to drive it without understanding how the gas pedal, steering wheel, and ignition switch worked. The same goes for your body and your partner's. Understanding the basic "switches and levers" is only going to enhance your intimate relationship.

THE NUTS AND BOLTS

We hope the chapter summaries have been helpful in allowing you to sample the basic concepts. That being said, if there were one chapter you should definitely read through, it would be this one!

This chapter took you through the basic anatomy and functions of the male and female genitalia. If you can't successfully define the words *labia, testes, perineum, vagina,* as well as others, then you need to spend some time in this chapter. After all, it's extremely important to understand what you're working with! Next, the chapter described the male and female arousal cycles—again, very crucial information if you desire a satisfactory physical relationship with your partner.

Our bodies are a wonderful paradox—simple and straightforward and yet complex and sophisticated at the same time. Understanding the way each gender is designed and functions is well-worth the short time it would take to read through the different definitions found in this chapter.

Chapter Questions for Real-Life Application

1. If you are not comfortable actually saying the names of the various body parts, go into a bathroom or bedroom, shut the door, and practice saying them until you feel more comfortable.

2. What new thing did you learn about your body or your partner's? Discuss it with each other.

3. Make a list of different ways you get "turned on" and share this list with your partner.

4. Does having a greater knowledge of your body and your partner's help you better understand his or her needs and wants? What changes could you make to further enhance your physical relationship?

4
UNDERSTANDING YOUR SEXUAL HISTORY

Identifying your own sexual history and development and how this impacts your relationship

IMAGINE YOU ARE TAKING A TRIP AND HEADING TO THE AIRPORT. With a suitcase and boarding pass in hand, you make your way to the security gate. You put your suitcase on the scanner and start making your way through the metal detector. This time, however, you don't know what's packed in your suitcase! You just picked it up and carried it around until it was time to go to the airport. Unfortunately, you never actually took the time to open it and see what might be in there. Oh, you have a general idea because you know your destination, and you assume the bag will have articles of clothing and toiletries appropriate for the climate and temperatures; but you have no idea about other items. What if there are prohibited liquids in your bag or items that would cause you embarrassment if you were the one selected to be searched?

Just like the suitcases we take with us on a trip, we all entered into our relationships carrying a suitcase and a story. The suitcases come in all different shapes, sizes, weights, textures, and fabrics, with a variety of items inside. Some of them are things we are comfortable and familiar with. We can easily share them with our spouse. However, other items may have shame or embarrassment attached. We can feel their weight, but we don't know what they are, or we're too scared to look at them.

Whatever kind of suitcase you have, it's safe to say we all entered into our marriages with baggage. And attached to it is a history.

Understanding your sexual history—or what is actually *in* your baggage—helps you know what you are bringing to your relationship. It gives you the opportunity to identify roadblocks as well as areas of strength and comfort. Without this knowledge, it is like traveling with a suitcase filled with explosives, and neither you nor your partner know when or what will set them off, leaving you both in a vulnerable situation.

So let's look at your story, starting with your childhood. Most parents don't realize they are teaching their children about sexuality the minute their children are born and begin changing diapers; kissing necks, ears, and toes; bathing them, and so on. Baby boys have erections within days of being born, and even in utero. Little girls have vaginas with a lot of folds and specific directions on how and which way to wipe them. Boys have a neat little appendage that is there for them to explore and play with while girls have something a little more vague, but no less interesting.

Children during potty training become even more intimately aware of their body parts—learning how they function and what they do—and became even more curious. It's amazing how up until around four years old, little kids won't think twice about being naked, bending over to have their bottom wiped, having their legs spread open as they are just playing and relaxing, and commenting on how their penis can grow and get big and then get small again. And these are just the lessons we learn in our first few years of life!

Now skip ahead as you started to develop breasts, pubic hair, and body odor and experienced your first wet dream or your period. How about the first time you rubbed up against something and noticed it felt good or had an innocent crush on the opposite sex? All of these naturally occurring phenomena were actually your foundational lessons in sexuality! Most of us might think that we learned about sex when our parents awkwardly sat us down to "have a talk," or during our fifth-grade maturation program, but really, how our parents responded to our bodies and the happenings, for better or worse, was our formative education in human sexuality. All these experiences added items to our suitcases—good and bad.

As we continued to grow, we started to notice more information and influences surrounding sexuality. Magazines, television, movies, and general media had all sorts of article teasers telling us what was supposedly "normal" for sexuality and selling the idea that, "if it's less than [fill in the blank]," then something was wrong with you, your partner, or your sexual relationship. In addition, we were also taught about sexuality at church and from our leaders. On an optimistic note, you may have been taught about all of the good things surrounding sexual intimacy and all the reasons to wait to share it with your spouse. Or maybe you learned, either directly or indirectly, that sex was "bad" or "taboo" while you were single and growing up, but once you married you would love it.

With this perspective, take a few moments to consider how various influences shaped your sexual story and education. Now consider how they shaped your spouse's sexual story and education. Have you ever had a conversation about what your spouse learned about sex and intimacy growing up? Not only is it tricky blending our life with another person, but blending our sexuality with our different backgrounds can be just as challenging. If you think you are having a physically intimate moment with just your spouse, think again. You are sharing that moment with your parents, your spouse's parents, and other friends and influences as well. Somehow you've got to make room in your suitcase for some of your spouse's stuff as well as sharing some of your stuff with your spouse. Those suitcases could get awfully heavy and bulky to carry around unless you figure out how to get rid of some of the unwanted or unneeded items. Just think about how liberating it would be to jettison unnecessary items and how much lighter and easier your relationship with each other could be. This would allow for greater understanding, compassion, and patience within your relationship!

Cody and Melissa

Cody came to the table with baggage he wasn't aware of. He had always had a desire to be appropriately physically intimate with girls he had dated. His recent engagement to Melissa was no different. Even though he was excited at the prospect of marriage, Cody was able to contain those powerful feelings and was content to wait until the appropriate time. Melissa, on the other hand, had a bit more of a sexual history and was looking forward to being able to be sexually intimate with Cody. As the wedding drew near, Cody started to express more apprehension regarding the honeymoon night. When they would talk about it, he would try to change the subject. Though Melissa noticed this, she thought it was just typical "first night" nerves.

However, after their temple sealing and on their way to the hotel room, Cody became increasingly nervous. Melissa, on the other hand, became increasingly excited and simply thought that she needed to help her new husband with performance anxiety and sex in general. What neither of the them knew was that Cody had been sexually abused when he was younger, and those memories had started to come forward. Cody felt guilty because he felt like he "should" want to have sex with his wife but felt scared and didn't actually like the idea of sex. Melissa took it personally and felt like he was personally rejecting her. She didn't understand that Cody's rejection of sex was not a rejection of Melissa, but of sex itself.

During their first year of marriage, the wedge between their sexual, physical, emotional, and spiritual intimacy gradually increased to the point where they decided they needed to seek help. Once they identified what was happening in their relationship—recognizing the baggage in their suitcases—they were able to start to dissolve the wedge and reconnect. By understanding what they were both bringing to the table—and Melissa discovered she had her own sexual baggage as well— they were able to further understand and support each other in a safe and intimate way.

While the above example contained trauma, sexual history isn't just about finding out about painful or traumatic experiences. In fact, statistically, less than half of adults will have experienced sexual trauma. But looking at what you learned about sex gives you greater understanding of yourself and your perspectives on sex.

It's important to realize we all have our "baggage." We bring this baggage into our relationships and the items contained inside affect our relationship for good or for bad. It takes courage, trust, and commitment to open our suitcase to our spouses and see what is inside. Actually looking at and handling the items inside can improve and strengthen our relationship in ways we couldn't have imagined before. You will feel more connected emotionally, spiritually, mentally, and physically with your spouse as you, together, begin to get rid of unwanted items, repack a few things, and even add a few items. Together you will begin to make a new suitcase filled with both the ups and downs of your relationship.

REAL RELATIONSHIP TIP!
Learning Something Painful about Your Spouse's Past

As you walk through your sexual histories, painful issues may be discovered. Many men and women have experiences of sexual abuse or molestation in their past and have carried this around—unspoken— for years. Others have engaged in sexual activities prior to marriage that they may feel shame or guilt for. If your spouse shares something with you, remember, though it may be hard for you to hear, it can feel very vulnerable, hard, and potentially scary to open up about these experiences. Listening with a soft heart while demonstrating compassion and love will be the best thing you can do. Suspending judgment and criticism is key. The Atonement not only covers sin, it heals the wounded heart and broken soul.

Now, a note to those of you who have been married for longer than a year: You may have added baggage, good or bad, due to the sexual experiences you've had together. It will still be good to go through the questions at the end of the chapter to discover if there is any area still affecting your relationship.

Linda and DJ

Linda, who had been married for eight years, recently learned about clitoral orgasm. For eight years, Linda had been acting as if she was really enjoying sex, but she was just doing what the magazines and movies all showed her she should be doing. Linda didn't really think sex was all that great and felt like it was more of a chore. Her husband, thinking Linda was having a great experience with sex, didn't think too much about it. When Linda was able to bring up the conversation with a girlfriend, the friend was astonished that Linda had never experienced an orgasm during her married years. She explained the process to Linda, who was more than embarrassed at the conversation, but also hopeful. Linda didn't want to talk to her husband about it because she felt like she had deceived him for years and didn't know how he'd react. However, Linda knew she wanted things to improve—not just for her, but for her husband as well. It was time to open that suitcase.

DJ, Linda's husband, felt stupid and embarrassed that he had not known this about Linda. In fact, he was mad for awhile. Soon, however, he realized that he too wanted their physical relationship to be as good as it could be and became excited at the prospect of learning more about sexuality together with Linda. They bought books, listened to seminars, and actually had a lot of fun re-experiencing this part of their relationship. They felt like newlyweds as Linda, for the first time, experienced an orgasm. Linda and DJ got rid of unwanted items from their suitcase and added some great ones that helped improve all areas of their relationship.

It may be helpful to realize that, even after a decade of marriage, there are still areas of sexuality about which you feel shame, fear, or resentment. Things may have happened during your marriage that haven't been understood and may have been hurtful. Take some time to reflect upon the sexual history of your own marriage and what things, if any, you need to remove from your suitcase or what items may need to be added. For good or for bad, taking a look at the sexual history of your relationship will create needed conversation and may even propel you forward into an even better and more meaningful experience.

THE NUTS AND BOLTS

Imagine you are taking a trip and heading to the airport. With suitcase and boarding pass in hand, you make your way to the security gate. You put your suitcase up on the scanner and start making your way through the metal detector. This time, however, you don't know what's packed in your suitcase! You just picked it up and carried it around until it was time to go to the airport, and, unfortunately, you never actually took the time to open it and see what might be in there. Oh, you have a general idea because you know your destination and you assume you will have clothing and toiletries appropriate for the climate and temperatures, but you have no idea about other items.

What if security finds items that would cause you embarrassment?

Just like the suitcases we take with us on a trip, we all entered into our relationship carrying a suitcase and a story. The suitcases come in all different shapes, sizes, weights, textures, and fabrics, with a variety of items inside. Some of them are things we are comfortable and familiar with. We can easily share them with our spouse. Other items may have shame or embarrassment attached—we can feel their weight but we don't know, or don't want to know, what they are. Whatever kind of suitcase you have, it's safe to say we all entered into our marriages with baggage. And attached to it is a history.

Understanding your sexual history—or what is actually *in* your baggage—helps you know what you are bringing to your relationship. It gives you the opportunity to identify roadblocks as well as areas of strength and comfort. Without this knowledge, it is like traveling with a suitcase filled with explosives, and neither you nor your partner knows when or what will set them off, leaving you both in a vulnerable situation.

Take a few moments to consider what you did and didn't learn about intimacy, and how that knowledge shaped your sexual story and education. Now consider what shaped your spouse's sexual story and education. Have you ever had a conversation with your spouse about what he learned about sex and intimacy growing up? Not only is it tricky blending our life with another person's, but blending our sexuality with our different backgrounds can be just as challenging. If you think you are having a physically intimate moment with just your spouse, think again. You are also influenced by parents, friends, society, and so on.

Somehow you've got to make room in your suitcase for some of your spouse's stuff as well as sharing some of your stuff with your spouse. Those suitcases could get awfully heavy and difficult to carry around unless you figure out how to get rid of some of the unwanted or unneeded items. Just think about how liberating it would be to jettison unnecessary items and how much lighter and easier your relationship with each other could be—it would allow for greater understanding, compassion, and patience.

Chapter Questions for Real-Life Application

So how do you start understanding what you are bringing to the table? Here are some questions to help you identify what's in your suitcase.

The questions for this chapter are intended to be used to gain more insight into each of you as individuals. Though you can work these questions together, it may be beneficial to answer these questions separately.

CHILDHOOD*

1. Describe the communication about sex in your home growing up. Who talked about sex? Who talked to whom? Who did not talk? What were your parents' attitudes about sex?
2. What memories do you have as a child about:
   Masturbation?
   Nudity?
   Sex play with siblings?
   Viewing sexually intimate behavior?
3. Did you experience sexual trauma as a child?

ADOLESCENCE*

1. As a teenager, did you masturbate? How did you feel about this?
2. What kinds of sexual behaviors did you engage in? How did you feel about this?
3. How did you feel about yourself and the opposite sex in your teen years?
4. What would you change if you could relive your adolescent sexual experiences?
5. What general attitudes and feelings did you have about sexuality in your adolescence?

ADULTHOOD*

1. Since you left your parents' home, how would you describe your sexual experiences, feelings, and definitions:
   In dating and relationships?
   In marriage?
   Alone?

MISCELLANEOUS QUESTIONS*

1. What was it like to be a girl or boy in your family during childhood, adolescence (puberty), and adulthood as it related to sexuality?
2. Who was most open sexually? Who was most closed?
3. How was sexuality viewed and talked about in your family?
4. What questions do you have regarding sexuality in your family that you have been reluctant to ask?
5. How could you discover the answers? Who might have the answers?
6. What do the other family members have to say regarding the above questions?
7. Who have you talked with about this? Who would you like to talk to about this?
8. What are the stories or myths and themes regarding sexuality in your family?

RELIGION*

1. What did you learn about sexuality growing up in your church?
2. What parts of your sexuality did you feel like you needed to keep a secret?
3. What did you learn about sexuality as a child?
4. What did you learn about sexuality as an adolescent?
5. What did you learn about sexuality on your honeymoon?
6. What did you learn about sexuality in marriage?
7. Did you or do you feel ashamed about any part of your sexuality?

CONCLUDING QUESTIONS

1. What new things did you learn about yourself as you went through your sexual history?
2. What things have you learned or experienced that have been strengths in your sexual relationship?
3. Were there any aspects of your history that make you feel ashamed or embarrassed? How do these influence your relationship and how you feel about yourself?

Written by and used with permission from Tina Schermer Sellers

5
HOW INTIMACY IS LIKE DINING

Sometimes we don't feel hungry, yet when we begin eating we realize we were hungrier than we thought

Dining Experience

THINK ABOUT ALL THE DIFFERENT DINING EXPERIENCES. SOME restaurants offer fast food, others offer seven-course meals—making for a slower experience, romantic conversation, and top customer service. Additionally, there are restaurants somewhere in-between, where you sit down or get take-out but still have an overall satisfying meal. There are convenience stores to satisfy a craving or a snack. Or perhaps you decide to go to a new restaurant for a completely new experience.

Intimacy is the same way. There is a variety of dining experiences we can have. Our lives, circumstances, and seasons in life influence the type of "dining" experiences we have presently and in the future. Hollywood would like us to believe that everyone is eating at five-star restaurants when it comes to sex and intimacy. If you aren't, *"What is wrong with you!"* Let's say you had the budget to eat at five-star restaurants each time you went out. Would you have the time? Would you even want to spend 2–3 hours a few times a week eating a fancy meal? Probably not. Having a fine-dining experience is nice every once in a while, but what about when you are hungry and only have time for the drive-thru?

Maybe you both have a favorite restaurant—like Chili's—you go to on your Friday date nights. It has something you both like on the menu, you can eat in a reasonable amount of time, and you leave feeling satisfied. Maybe you just had a baby and for the next year you are mostly getting take-out intimate experiences sprinkled with the occasional fancy meal. When you do have a babysitter, you're able to go to Chili's where you both love to go. The bottom line is to allow your relationship to be open to a variety of intimate experiences. There are almost unlimited dining choices. It's important to be creative and adaptable regarding your intimacy. In other words, broaden your menu.

Cuisine

How did we learn what our food preferences were? Have they always remained the same? Have we ever obtained a preference for a new food or a new way to cook or present the food? Just because we didn't like something at fourteen, do we allow that early preference to affect how we see that same thing at thirty? Because your wife did not like the food one night, do we then generalize that to mean we must never present it to her again? Because we did not like the pizza at one place, does that mean we will never try it if we visit Italy?

Think of all the different types of cuisine that are available: Chinese, American, Italian, Greek—and that's just the beginning! Within each of these types of dining exist even more variations. Intimacy is like the different foods we like to eat. We have our favorites, our not-so-favorites, the food that makes us nauseated just thinking about, and the foods we are willing to eat from time to time (like grandma's bean casserole!)—but please, not every day. Think about the last time you had a meal that you didn't really like. Did you boycott eating entirely because you ate one thing you didn't like? Did you decide that you did not like the way it tasted but still enjoyed eating all your other favorite foods? With intimacy, if you have an experience or try something that you don't like, do you boycott intimacy or your spouse altogether? Do you decide that because you didn't like one experience, you don't like sexual intimacy? What about a new and different food that didn't excite you initially, but you learned to like over time? How about that possibility with a sexual or emotional experience?

The variety of intimate and sexual possibilities—like food—can be both positive and negative. We learn about our food preferences because we have many opportunities throughout a day, week, or year to learn about what we like and dislike—because we continue eating. We don't say, "Because I didn't like that food, I will now only have grilled cheese for the rest of my life." Most of us continue to be open to experiences—for better or worse—to develop our preferences, tastes, dislikes, and favorites and to learn more about our partner and ourselves!

The Need to Eat

We have a need to eat to be healthy and functional. Food provides energy, impacts our mood, affects our ability to think, and fuels us to be able to participate in life. Similarly, intimacy is a fundamental foundation of our relationship—referring to the intimacy pyramid—providing connection, security, chemicals that cause closeness, attachment, and well-being. Sexual activity, in particular, also provides ongoing improvement in our ability not to feel alone in this world. Then there are the many health benefits such as relieving stress, reducing depression, improving self-esteem, and providing a feeling of mutual love.

Can you imagine going days without food, let alone weeks or months? How would your energy be? How would your mood be? How would your ability to focus, concentrate, and work be? Now we're not suggesting that we need sex to sustain life, but we can relate these above-mentioned benefits to sex. Sex is not simply something that is a "perk" of a relationship; it's a necessary and important factor. Consider how a sexless or a sexually strained relationship affects the way you feel about yourself, your spouse, your marriage, how you treat your children, or how you approach your job. Emotional and spiritual deprivation is the same way. You could certainly survive a marriage with low or little intimacy, but it will not thrive and will be relationally lethargic.

Hungry versus Not-Hungry Factor

Hunger is another factor that is crucial when it comes to eating. Ideally, you and your spouse are both hungry and eager to enjoy a good meal. However, it may also be that you or your partner have varying appetites and don't realize the other is hungry until you sit down to eat. There may have been times in your relationship where you just weren't very hungry. Your partner was starving, however, so you chose to join him or her in a meal. Apply the hunger analogy to sex: you may both be hungry, or it may take you starting to be intimate to realize you really were hungrier than you thought. Maybe you weren't necessarily hungry, but you weren't opposed to dining. And then there are understandably going to be times when you just don't feel like eating at all.

These experiences are all a natural part of a healthy sexual relationship with many factors contributing to the overall appetites of you and your spouse. If your spouse said he wasn't hungry one night, would you take it personally? Would you take offense at it? Would it cause a fight? Would you invite him to dinner another night or look at his day or circumstances and consider these factors in connection with his lack of being "hungry"? So much weight and discussion are placed on the low-versus-high appetite within a marriage. Look at how often your appetite changes and varies over the course of your life.

When there is latitude regarding our intimate appetites, it frees us from only being allowed to "feel hungry or else" in our relationships. Sometimes we can just be happy for the other's desire and be grateful that he still wants to be with us—that we are still attractive to him, that she is fulfilled by being close to us. We need to get ourselves out of the way at times and be content that our spouse loves and wants us. "Hunger" for another person is a beautiful thing. Can we learn to, at times, be okay that we are being served up for the other person to enjoy and feel satisfied? Can we alter our needs to allow ourselves to enjoy being wanted, desired, and loved by this other person?

When Your Appetites Don't Mesh at All

Literally speaking, if you ask women when the most challenging time to eat is, most would say during the first months of pregnancy and the first year postpartum. It may not be only eating, but it may be meal planning, grocery shopping, or cooking—anything to do with food. For some women, if food is made and they are able to eat it, they are happy because they didn't have to exert the mental energy that goes into making, planning, and preparing the meal. Yet women need to eat during those times because it can decrease their nausea and increase their much-needed physical energy to get through their day.

There may be times when a woman doesn't feel like meeting any other person's needs any longer. She doesn't want a baby sucking on her, touching her, needing her energy, or imploring her to listen and care for him. She is overwhelmed and tired. Then her husband comes home. She has not had time to even shower. She feels gross, dirty, sticky, worn, and the need to just be left alone. As she stands in the kitchen, getting the night bottle ready, her husband touches her painful breast and suggests, "Hey, I know, I'll meet you in the shower!" What to do? What to say? Should she laugh? Cry? Throw up? Scream? What?

Meghan and Cory

Meghan and Cory have been married for eight months. They have a cute apartment in the city, and both Meghan and Cory work within ten minutes of their home. For the past few months they started meeting each other at home to have lunch together just to connect during their busy days. On this particular lunch date, Cory had just come from a really stressful meeting with his boss and was feeling a bit overwhelmed. Meghan initiated sex, which was something that was not unusual. While the kissing was passionate and the feelings were all there, Cory could not get a full erection. Despite both of them wanting to have sexual intercourse, it just wasn't going to happen. Cory felt horrible and believed something was wrong, yet Meghan lovingly replied, "Hey, it's okay. This was just Wednesday afternoon sex. It doesn't mean that all our sexual experiences—or even our lunch-time experiences—will be like this. It doesn't even mean something is wrong with you. It just means this was our experience for today at this moment."

Can you see how differently this could have played out for this couple? Many days of pain, bad memories, and shame have started with the exact same scenario. It is a sad fact that our brains are hard-wired to remember what goes wrong far more than what goes well. To use the food analogy again, we can eat ninety-nine times at a particular restaurant and enjoy every meal. On the hundredth time, we eat a fish taco and get terribly sick—up all night, on the toilet, so sick we cannot see straight. So does our mind remember the ninety-nine good experiences? Or does this one awful experience overwhelm all the good times we have had at that favorite restaurant?

This correlates with sexual not-so-good experiences in marriage and relationships. One bad erection, illness, or outcome can color many lost possibilities because we become afraid that the poor outcome will reoccur and that we will be powerless over it. The only way to fix bad outcomes is to overwhelm them with good outcomes through practice, communication, and loving kindness and concern about the well-being of our partner.

More often than not, you just need a little help diffusing your emotions—and physical intimacy is fraught with emotion. By comparing sex to dining, and doing the above exercise, you will be able to move to a place less overwhelming, complicated, emotional, or painful, and move to understanding, laughter, forgiveness, and growth.

Throughout this book, we will refer to the "sex is like dining" analogy. We'll use different examples and illustrations of how using this tool can help keep your relationship in perspective and an endeavor worth pursuing.

(If you find yourself having repeated experiences that aren't working or that you are not "eating," check out our chapter on professional help.)

THE NUTS AND BOLTS

In this chapter, we offered you a great analogy having to do with something we can all relate to—food. We compared physical intimacy to our physical appetite and desire for food. Yes, without food we would literally starve and die—which isn't the case with physical intimacy. However, a relationship can be greatly affected and seem to be "starving" due to a lack of physical intimacy within it.

First, think of how you went about learning about your food preferences. You tried some things and liked them instantly. Other things you tried and hated. You may have turned your nose up to a few things at first, but, with time, learned to actually enjoy them. Additionally, just because you may have had a bad experience with your grandma's goulash doesn't mean you stopped eating forever! It just means you learned to avoid goulash whenever possible and let your spouse know you would prefer not to eat it.

Second, think of how many kinds of restaurants there are and the wide variety of food and atmospheres—anywhere from drive-thru to a seven-course meal. There is just as much potential variety within a physical relationship. If it would be boring to just have one restaurant, with one kind of food option, think of how that applies to a physical relationship.

Third, our appetites are constantly changing. Sometimes we are famished. Other times we would like something light and quick. Sometimes we barely have time for anything but a donut at the Qwik Mart. During times of ill health, pregnancy, or stress, our appetites may greatly diminish. In addition, while we may be super hungry, our spouse may not be hungry at all at the moment. The trick is learning to mesh the two into something workable, functional, and healthy. Just as you wouldn't take it personally if your spouse weren't hungry, you also wouldn't manipulate her into eating an entire meal just because you want one. On the other hand, she may agree to go with you to the restaurant and order something light while you order a large entree. And so on . . .

This analogy can apply to every aspect of our physical relationship. It helps give you a way to talk about things going on in your sexual relationship without becoming defensive, getting hurt, accusing, or feeling guilty. Our physical relationship can become so emotionally charged, it's difficult to discuss anything without it turning into a disaster. This analogy takes off and can bring you to a place where actual discussion can take place. It will also help you to see your partner, or your physical relationship, in a different light.

Chapter Questions for Real-Life Application

1. How would you describe your sexual appetite? How is it different from your spouse's?

2. Do you have a type of "dining" experience you prefer? Compare with your spouse. You may be surprised at what you find out.

3. Is there a different "dining experience" you'd like to try? Describe it.

4. Think of a bad "dining experience"—we've all had them. Is this experience still affecting your intimate relationship?

6

BOUNDARIES—WHERE
I END AND YOU BEGIN

And how this contributes to a
stronger, healthier relationship

ODDLY ENOUGH, A HUGE BARRIER TO TRUE AND LASTING INTI-
macy is a lack of healthy self-esteem and boundaries. Although
we speak of "becoming one" in a marriage, it's important to
define what that really means for the individuals involved. You can
spend a lot of time and effort working to improve communication and
change behaviors, but without a clear understanding of who you are
and what you bring to the relationship, you may feel like all your hard
work isn't getting you anywhere.

You bring unique needs, complexities, and wants to your relationship—as does your spouse. Addressing and working on creating a
healthy self-esteem and boundaries makes conversations more meaningful, increases positive interactions, and makes conflict purposeful
and productive—yes, there is a place for conflict within a relationship. As you strive to balance your intimacy pyramid, obtaining and
maintaining your sense of self is like adding a scaffolding around the
outside—providing extra support and stability throughout the process.

Boundaries—A Wall or Map?

Okay, now that we've tossed this word around quite a bit, let's
actually figure out the meaning. The word "boundaries" is a buzz word

frequently used in conversations but is a difficult concept for many. A man recalled, as a missionary in a foreign country, giving an entire talk using a word he thought meant "to procrastinate." After the talk many people approached him to thank him for his words of advice, recognizing they should avoid doing what he said, but they told him there wasn't a word in their language for what he described and didn't know to what he was referring! To them it sounded like gibberish.

To create and maintain boundaries, you need to clearly understand the concept. A boundary is not a wall you build around yourself to keep your spouse out. Instead, think of it like the boundary lines drawn on a map. It's clear where one state or country begins and another ends. However, on the ground there aren't any actual lines—just a simple sign indicating you have entered or left a distinct area and have now crossed over. The roads, signs, and local culture may be different and things aren't going to change simply because you entered the territory. Nor are you going to drastically change yourself to better fit in the new area just because you are visiting.

In Robert Frost's poem "Mending the Wall," he says, "Good fences make good neighbors." When we understand where our "boundary line" is and that of our spouse, feelings of trust, safety, and understanding—the elements of the scaffolding—thrive. You will then know and be able to communicate your needs and wants without blurring them into your spouse's. Your spouse will be able to share his hopes and desires without you taking responsibility to fulfill them all. This will enable you to actually meet your spouse's needs better, and the "behaviors" you've been trying to change can begin to work themselves out.

Lexi and Matt and Matt's Mother, Donna

Lexi and Matt hadn't been married long when they went to Matt's parents' home for dinner one Sunday. During dessert, Matt's mother brought up the subject of children and asked when Lexi and Matt were "going to get started" having babies? Lexi just smiled and said she and Matt were figuring out their plan and would be sure to let Matt's parents know when and if a baby was on the way. Donna, however, wasn't about to let the subject drop and pressed them for more information concerning their finances and thoughts about birth control. At this point Matt stepped in. He nicely, but pointedly, told his mother that his and Lexi's decisions were "their" decisions and not hers. While they appreciated her interest and hoped their future children would have a great relationship with their grandma, they weren't going to discuss all their important decisions with her. Donna was surprised but satisfied by this response. She was better able to see Lexi and Matt as autonomous and developed a newfound respect for both her son and daughter-in-law. Lexi appreciated Matt creating this boundary with his mother and resolved to do the same with her parents, as well as others, to protect the relationship she and Matt were building.

This example illustrates how a married couple creates boundaries for their relationship but applies to the individual as well. Neither Matt nor Lexi became emotional or upset by the line of questioning. They both held their ground while maintaining the relationship with Matt's mother. Furthermore, neither Matt nor Lexi felt responsible for Donna's emotions or reactions but allowed her to have her own experience with the conversation. The relationship between the three of them was actually strengthened and enhanced because each was able to remain autonomous. The new feeling of respect allowed adult interactions to take place instead of childish, destructive moments.

Differentiation—Who I Am Is Good Enough

When we are able to see ourselves—strengths, weaknesses, idiosyncrasies, and so on—as separate and of worth, we are "differentiated." It's knowing our worth is not dependent on our successes, outside praise, or doing "good" or "bad" things—it simply is. Continuing with our map analogy, the province of Quebec, Canada, is unique because the primary language spoken is French. The rest of Canada primarily speaks English. Quebec doesn't apologize for its differences nor does it think it's less valuable than the other provinces. It's simply Quebec. If you visit Quebec, you go with the knowledge French will be spoken.

When our self-worth is poor, we rely heavily on the approval of others to make up the difference. Sometimes the need becomes so great that we do things to fill an impossible void in such a manner. We may employ tactics such as control, manipulation, or utter compliance to maintain a false sense of peace within the relationship. A marriage cannot thrive under such circumstances. Leading couples' therapist David Schnarch describes differentiation as it relates to intimacy this way: "The person with the least desire for intimacy always controls intimacy in the relationship as long as partners are dependent on validation from each other." Quebec and the other Canadian provinces are able to work together, despite their differences, for the betterment of their country while maintaining their unique qualities.

Pia Mellody says it best, "Human beings have their limitations, but these limitations are not faults; they simply are a part of the given truth about humans. If we learn to despise ourselves for being limited humans, we lost contact with the prime spiritual truth of our reality: that we are not perfect and this is all right." In fact, not only is it all right, but it is all part of God's plan. It's through our planned imperfection that we become reliant on the Atonement that ultimately fosters the humility necessary to learn and grow. Doctrine and Covenants 18:47 reminds us to "Remember the worth of souls is great in the sight of God." Period. Our worth is an undeniable, eternal truth. Our job is to believe this truth and live accordingly.

The Adult Tantrum—It's Not Pretty

A lyric from a famous song states, "Act your age, not your shoe size!" As adults, we like to think we have moved beyond the stage of screaming, flailing about, or stomping our feet when we don't get something we want. At times, babies and toddlers act this way because they are developmentally unable to clearly express calmly and rationally their needs and wants. They become overwhelmed by their emotions and fall to the floor crying. Believe it or not, adults still engage in tantrum-like behavior even though they are developmentally capable of clearly communicating. The capacity is there, but we often lack the skills and knowledge necessary to truly act like a "grown-up." Our tantrums are more subtle and sophisticated—meaning we probably aren't rolling around on the floor kicking and screaming. Behaviors such as punishing, withdrawing, entitlement, superiority, and belittling are just a few of the ways we may be trying to get our needs met in a "childish" way. If we or our spouse are not fully differentiated, we can inadvertently engage in behaviors that will perpetuate the tantrums and create a cycle of over-accommodating, walling off, or throwing our own tantrum—all of which are barriers to intimacy.

Hundreds of articles have been written about how to handle a toddler's tantrum. We are to do things like ignore him; place the child in "time out" if necessary; and console a little bit to reassure, but we must not give in to the behavior. This same advice applies to adult tantrums. When we own our thoughts and feelings and allow our spouse to own hers, we avoid entering the tantrum-cycle. We maintain the relationship and quality of intimacy while effectively working through differences of opinion, misunderstandings, and painful situations. Mastering this skill requires time and effort but will free you from the whining child inside and instead help you become the confident adult you want to be.

Sharon and Derek

When Sharon first married Derek, her perception of their roles was that she was the "princess" and Derek the "groveling peasant." Sharon would often use manipulation and punishment to get what she wanted from Derek. Over time Derek grew tired of his "station" and started withdrawing emotionally. The more he withdrew, the more Sharon did as well until they were both figuratively "kicking and screaming" on the floor with neither knowing what to do about it.

Feeling sad and lonely, Sharon attended a class about raising self-esteem, thinking she was going to be told how she "deserved to be happy" and how her husband should be doing more to make her happy. What she got was the complete opposite. She was told that self-worth was not to be dependent on your spouse, your family, or the world, but that self-worth came from God and understanding your own unique qualities. The class continued on in the same vein, and Sharon said she felt like she had been "slapped in the face." But it was a good and necessary slap, waking her up to the mess she had helped create.

She left the class with a better grasp of her role in her marital conflict and vowed to make changes—starting with apologizing to Derek for the way she had treated him and for expecting him to build her feelings of self-worth. That Friday night Sharon was looking forward to spending time with Derek but knew there was a big football game he was excited to watch. Sharon watched the game with Derek for awhile but then told him she was going to bed. She hoped he would come along, but he decided to finish watching the game.

When Derek finally came to bed, Sharon expressed her disappointment that they weren't able to spend more time together but this time didn't use any sort of punishment or manipulation to try to make him "help her feel better." When the next weekend rolled around, Derek went out of his way to schedule a date with Sharon—causing him to miss a football game. They had a great talk about their needs and wants without resorting to any tantrum-like behaviors. Their individual confidence and feelings of self-worth increased, which then deepened and strengthened their intimacy.

When you were a baby, your caretakers met all your needs. If you were hungry, they fed you. If you needed cuddling, they held you. If you wanted entertainment, they made funny faces. When you expect your spouse or others to constantly meet all your needs, you are acting in an infantile state instead of an adult-partnership state. Society has made this more difficult by bombarding us with messages with the phrases, "You deserve _____! You're entitled to _____! You shouldn't have to _____!" These false ideas resonate with the toddler in us and stifle the emergence of the adult. Marriage is an adult concept. If you want a healthy, functional marriage, you must learn to "act your age and not your shoe size!"

REAL RELATIONSHIP TIP!
Let's Find the "U" and "I" in UnIty

Hollywood sells the idea that true love and passion is when two people sacrifice their own identities and meld into one. Couples get cute, blended names such as "Brangelina," where they are no longer two individuals but one unit—this is a mark of love! A healthy relationship has two individuals who are able to connect and disengage with flexibility. When we move to the extreme with our connectedness or disengagement, we move out of functional relating and into dysfunctional relating and patterns. While it seems appealing and safe to be each other's entire world, relationships can quickly sour and often dissolve completely from suffocation.

PIA MELLODY'S RELATIONSHIP MAXIMS*

You cannot "nice" someone into a relationship—being real in a relationship and being nice are very different. Being nice is a mask and does not offer truth and intimacy—it is non-relational.

You can't be distant and caring. When you care for someone, you are there for that person. Show up and be present, otherwise distance will prevail. Care often involves a hands-on approach.

If you are judgmental, your value system may be too big. People with a big value system tend to look at people who see things differently as "bad" rather than different. They put themselves in a "one-up" position in order to look down on all the wrong people. In the end, we are left with a big value system and a small number of friends.

Our own experience of shame makes it possible to be relational. When you accept your own humanness and imperfection, you are less likely to judge and will be more humble. Humility is recognizing both our strengths and weaknesses.

We choose our behavior. The world chooses our consequences. We cannot control how our actions will be received by others. We surrender the right to decide that when in a relationship. Choosing to be authentically present is all we can choose.

When walled-in people develop healthy boundaries, they will at first feel naked and vulnerable. You cannot connect with people if you are hiding behind walls in relationships, nor can other people connect with you. It's isolating and lonely. When you start pulling down the walls you were familiar with, it can feel very uncomfortable. But it will get better.

Resentment is like taking poison in the hope that your enemy will die. Resentment and self-pity are important when we feel someone has wronged us and treated us as if we were worthless. Resentment and self-pity help us go to a proper defense. But when we falsely feel that we are victims, and when we feel the need to get even with someone who has not victimized us, we become obnoxious and self-defeating.

Getting esteem from someone else never creates self-esteem. Self-esteem comes from inside of ourselves. It does not waver and holds strong in the face of judgement of others. The esteem that comes from praise from other people is called other-esteem and varies from person to person.

Setting up boundaries with those who are boundary-less makes them feel abandoned. People who don't have boundaries generally get too close and overstep others' spaces. If you place a boundary on them, they feel threatened, no matter how healthy the boundary. The opposite is true as well. Those who have walls for boundaries will feel naked when the wall is removed and feel very vulnerable with appropriate boundaries in place.

adapted or directly quoted from Pia Mellody's book, The Intimacy Factor, *pgs. 135–138. Used with permission.*

Intimacy Is Not for the Faint of Heart

When you learn how to self-regulate and tolerate your own emotions as well as your spouse's, change starts to happen. Movement happens. The scaffolding is built and your intimacy pyramid begins to stabilize, balance, and grow. You are able to clearly express your needs and wants in a healthy and direct way with the understanding that you may not always get what you want. Your spouse is able to genuinely respond with honesty and sincerity instead of fear or anger. You are able to remain true to yourself and honor your spouse's individuality, too. Your capacity for intimacy will continue to increase as you continue to refine this skill.

True adult intimacy moves us from a state of reaction to a state of action. It moves us into choosing to love our spouse, choosing to meet his needs when possible, and choosing to remain in the relationship—identifying and expressing our needs at the same time. Creating and honoring functional boundaries and developing a healthy self-worth can be a difficult and painful work, but it will prove to be the most lasting and satisfying work you will do in your relationship. When we open ourselves to our spouse—strengths and weaknesses—we invite our relationship to become deeper and more intimate then previously imagined. In Shakespeare's words, "To thine own self be true."

If you find yourself or your relationship repeating patterns of the adult-tantrum cycle and find it difficult to change, you may need extra help in the self-worth and boundaries area. For further guidance, please see our resource section.

THE NUTS AND BOLTS

This chapter discussed why creating and maintaining a healthy line around yourself and your marriage protects and enhances intimacy.

Oddly enough, a huge barrier to true and lasting intimacy is a lack of healthy self-esteem and boundaries. Although we speak of "becoming one" in a marriage, it's important to define what that really means for the individuals involved. You can spend a lot of time and effort working to improve communication and change behaviors, but without a clear understanding of who you are and what you bring to the relationship, you may feel like all your hard work isn't getting you anywhere.

To create and maintain boundaries, you need to clearly understand the concept. A boundary is not a wall you build around yourself to keep your spouse out. Instead, think of it like the boundary lines drawn on a map. It's clear where one state or country begins and another ends. However, on the ground there aren't any actual lines, but there may be a simple sign indicating you have entered or left a distinct area and have now crossed over. The roads, signs, and local culture may be different, and things aren't going to change simply because you entered the territory. Nor are you going to drastically change yourself to better fit in the new area just because you are visiting.

When we are able to see ourselves—strengths, weaknesses, idiosyncrasies, and so on—as separate and of worth, we are "differentiated." It's knowing our worth is not dependent on our successes, outside praise, or doing "good" or "bad" things—it simply is. When our self-worth is poor, we rely heavily on the approval of others to make up the difference. Sometimes the need becomes so great that we do things to fill an impossible void in such a manner. We may employ tactics such as control, manipulation, or utter compliance to maintain a false sense of peace within the relationship. A marriage cannot thrive under such circumstances.

A lyric from a famous song states, "Act your age, not your shoe size!" Believe it or not adults still engage in tantrum-like behavior even though they are developmentally capable of clearly communicating. The capacity is there, but we often lack the skills and knowledge necessary to truly act like a grown-up. Our tantrums are more subtle and sophisticated—meaning we probably aren't rolling around on the floor kicking and screaming. Behaviors such as punishing, withdrawing, entitlement, superiority, and belittling are just a few of the ways we use to get our needs met in a "childish" way. If we or our spouse are not fully differentiated, we can inadvertently engage in behaviors that will perpetuate the tantrums and create a cycle of over-accommodating, walling off, or throwing our own tantrum—all of which are barriers to intimacy.

When you learn how to self-regulate and tolerate your own emotions as well as your spouse's, change starts to happen. Movement happens. Scaffolding is built and your intimacy pyramid begins to stabilize, balance, and grow. You can clearly express your needs and wants in a healthy and direct way with the understanding that you may not always get what you want. Your spouse is able to genuinely respond with honesty and sincerity instead of fear or anger. You are able to remain true to yourself and honor your spouse's individuality too. Your capacity for intimacy will continue to increase as you continue to refine this skill.

Chapter Questions for Real-Life Application

1. Consider the source of your feelings of self-worth:
    from others?
    from doing things to receive praise?
    from God?

2. Which way feels the most sincere and lasting? Ask Heavenly Father if He'll let you see yourself how He sees you and notice how that knowledge changes your perspective on yourself, your spouse, and those around you.

3. Take one week and note all of the ways you throw "sophisticated tantrums" to get your needs met. What tactics do you employ? What are you wanting or needing but indirectly asking for?

4. What has been your experience with boundaries growing up? Do you find that you relate to your spouse in a similar way?

7

CREATING THE CONVERSATION

*How to talk about sex and intimacy
in your relationship*

HERE YOU ARE. WE HOPE YOU HAVE A BETTER UNDERSTANDING of what intimacy is all about. You may even have an idea of where your relationship is strong, where you could improve, or where you even need a complete overhaul. But this is where it gets tricky! It's that whole relationship piece again, and you may be realizing that you and your spouse need to have some conversations. For some couples, these may be the first conversations they will have had—with positive or even negative associations.

For some of you, these types of conversations have happened but have tended to end up in a fight. For others, you have talked about having the conversation but never get around to it or don't know how to really go as deeply as you'd like. Maybe you avoid the topic altogether and are starting from square one. Possibly it's a matter of pushing through the embarrassment and vulnerability, and you don't quite know where to start. No matter where you are, you can start having conversations with your spouse.

Remember your first sexual encounter with your spouse and all of the feelings that came with it? With more experiences and exposure to physical intimacy, you both probably became more comfortable and the various anxieties died down. These conversations are much the same way. There is a learning curve, with lots of fumbles and wrong turns. However, if you keep your goal in mind, you can navigate everything that comes your way.

Returning to the mountain landscape analogy, having a broad perspective about conversation can make or break the tone, understanding, and outcome. First, you need to be honest with yourself and identify where you are coming from. Are you frustrated? Are you angry? Are you looking to understand as well as be understood? Are you wanting to vent and not necessarily looking to have a conversation, but hoping to have a validating sounding board? What are you hoping to get out of the conversation? An apology? An action item? A new sense of understanding? Inviting your partner to try something new? Knowing where you are coming from and what you hope to gain from the conversation gives the conversation a chance to have a positive outcome and a platform to have more conversations.

Perspective Check

Let's do a little exercise on perspective. Ideally, you would do this with your spouse, but you can also do it alone. Find a room to sit in, preferably one you aren't overly familiar with. On a piece of paper, jot down what you notice about the room. Have your spouse do the same. It can be furniture items, the smell, the shape, and so on. Now share with your partner what you noticed and ask him to share his list too. After you have both had the opportunity to share, identify whose description is more accurate or correct. You may have found this to be a challenge—and in fairness to you, it's a trick question. Though you are both sharing your description of the same room, what you notice and experience with that room will be different. Can you imagine what a conversation would look like as you tried to prove whose description of the room was more correct? Now take your descriptions of the room and rather than trying to prove who is more accurate, attempt to learn how your partner experiences the room, what she notices. There's not a right or wrong with this exercise, just an opportunity to learn.

The first conversation would look much like two lawyers in a courtroom without a judge, both trying to prove the other wrong with little listening or understanding and a lot of frustration and tension. This is what often happens when we have conversations about sex, money, and children. We find ourselves trying to prove whose experience with the situation is right, missing the opportunity to learn more about our spouse and how he sees the situation. When it comes to intimacy and sex, you are both experiencing it differently and *both* experiences are valid. The key to these conversations is to move from lawyers on opposing sides to teammates with a common interest. With these keys in mind, here are some ways to move from tension to connection when talking about sex and intimacy.

Be Honest with Yourself

As we mentioned earlier, you need to understand where you are coming from and what you hope to get from the conversation. Whether it's to share an idea and not wanting feedback or to vent a frustration, knowing where you are coming from and communicating that up front to your spouse so he understands where you are coming from can facilitate meaningful conversation.

Invite the Spirit

Prior to approaching your spouse, consider consulting with Heavenly Father. It can help soften your heart, give you further clarity with the situation, and allow for the Spirit to facilitate your conversation. This also is another way to include the Lord in your relationship, therein fostering spiritual intimacy.

Timing, Timing, Timing

We have all had conversations where we were tired and hungry and the outcome was less than positive simply because of the timing of bringing up the topic. Timing can be 90 percent of the solution. Find a time where you are both fed and rested, ideally not distracted or under significant stress. Keep in mind when we are facing something that challenges us, we may put it off by waiting for the perfect time; however, that perfect time may never happen. Whether it's waiting for a better (not perfect) time or creating time, timing is key. Consider having a weekly check-in with your spouse where you specifically discuss how things are going for you each of you relating to intimacy.

Start with What's Working

By starting with what you enjoy, appreciate, love, and respect, your partner feels that you see her as a whole person, with strengths and weaknesses. It's easy to get into a trap of only sharing with our spouse areas of frustration. When you develop the habit of pointing out positives, your spouse will be more inclined to receive what you are saying. Who doesn't appreciate hearing positive things about himself? Things you want to communicate are:

I love you

I want to feel closer to you than I do

I want you to be able to trust me and be confident in your feelings for me

I want us to feel safe and comfortable with each other

I want to share all kinds of intimacy with you and be your true partner

These are the strengths I see in you . . .

Own Your Perspective

When addressing an issue, understand that simply because you feel a certain way doesn't mean that it's truth. It's simply your experience with the situation. One way we own our perspective is to move away from blame and "you always do this" statements to "I feel like this" or "this is my experience." This can help keep a conversation from becoming emotionally charged because your spouse isn't having to prepare his rebuttal. Again, this moves you out of a potential debate to a place of understanding and emotional intimacy.

Be a Curious Listener

Think of the common question, "How was your day?" The typical response is "good." A curious listener inquires about what made your day good and asks, "What made it good?" Being a curious listener will get you more information and reduce assumption—often mistaken—of how your partner feels, which then reduces further misunderstandings. The act of curiosity in a conversation also shows an inherent interest and desire to understand where the other is coming from.

Stay on Topic

It's tempting when we have a window of opportunity to talk meaningfully with our spouse to start unloading all of the things that bother, annoy, or downright make us angry. When this happens, it can naturally cause our spouse to become defensive, and a conversation quickly turns from potentially constructive to destructive. This can also relate to your couple intimate history. You may have a current experience that hurt you and during the conversation start bringing up all of the other times where she has hurt you in the same way. If you find this happening often, consider seeking professional help. The counselor or coach can help you identify the root of why the same issue continues to come up and find healthy solutions.

Physical Touch

Simple physical touch during a conversation can also soften the tone. Whether it's putting your hand on her hand or sitting with knees touching, physical touch can connect you as you discuss potentially difficult matters.

Consider Professional Help

If you find you are having repeated conversations that turn into heated arguments or if neither of you feels you are getting anywhere, consider seeking professional help. See our chapter "Professional Help" to see times when it may be a good idea to see a counselor or coach.

REAL RELATIONSHIP TIP!
Anger Cool Down

Inevitably, every couple has arguments—some more heated than others. It's safe to say that hardly anything is accomplished until you both take a break and calm down. Research has provided an answer for this: anger resides in the reptilian—or more primitive area—of the brain, as well as our flight-or-fight instincts. This part of our brain is unable to produce rational, productive, and logical thought. Can you recall a time when you've been angry and rational at the same time? Unfortunately, it's during these times we say and do things we wouldn't consider under normal circumstances because our "thinking" brain has been shoved out of the way by our primitive instinct to "survive" and avoid pain at all costs—despite the cost to our spouse and relationship. Unless you take a few deep breaths, take a break from the conversation, or implement some other "cool down" strategies, you literally cannot engage your rational and productive self. You are arguing from survival mode. So, before your next argument, here are a few tips you can use to remain civil and respectful instead of hurtful and irrational:

Take a break. If you find your conversation becoming heated and are becoming increasingly angry, take a break and revisit the issue once you're both calm. Own that you are angry and need to take a break.

State a time that you would like to revisit the conversation and try again.

Go for a walk. Going for a brisk walk can give your body, mind, and emotions a much needed break and help release pent-up emotion.

Breathe. Taking slow, deep, breaths slows your heart rate and helps bring you to a calmer state. Put your palm on your stomach and take slow deep breaths—in and out—and repeat as needed.

Engage your senses. Find things appealing to your senses that help you to relax. This may be listening to some relaxing music, visualizing yourself at your favorite spot—like the beach—or aromatherapy. Persistent and heated anger is counter to cultivating intimacy and creating a sense of safety in a marriage. If you have difficulty managing your anger, are on the receiving end of someone who cannot control his anger, or are involved in an abusive situation, seek professional help and ecclesiastical support.

THE NUTS AND BOLTS

Approaching a conversation on intimacy with your spouse can feel as potentially intimidating or daunting as your first sexual encounter. However, with a few basic skills, gleaned from this chapter, you will feel more confident and willing to begin having these conversations. A major premise in this chapter is that although you are involved in an intimate relationship with someone else, you are also having your own unique experience with it. Arguing about whose experience is right, wrong, or more justified is like two attorneys in a courtroom, without a judge. By being willing to understand your spouse's point of view, you both get a clear picture of what's really going on. Be sure to check out the Perspective Check exercise in the chapter.

Here are some things to consider as you approach a conversation about intimacy:

1) Be honest about where you are coming from. Are you angry and just needing to vent? Are you looking for a reciprocal conversation? Are you looking to problem solve?

2) Invite the Spirit to be a part of your conversation. The Holy Ghost can soften, clarify, and help facilitate the conversation.

3) Consider your timing. At a minimum, it's a good idea to make sure you are both fed and rested. Rather than wait for the perfect opportunity to present itself to address your intimacy, create a good time where you can both be present.

4) Start with what's working. By identifying what your partner's strengths are and the positives in your relationship, you are more likely to have a partner who will receive and be open to what you have to say.

5) Own your perspective. Remember, your experience with your relationship is your experience and may not be what your spouse feels. Avoid blaming and using "You always" or "You never." Instead use "I feel" or "This is how I see the situation."

6) Be a curious listener. Being a curious listener will get you more information and reduce assumptions about how your partner feels, which then reduces further misunderstandings. The act of curiosity in a conversation also shows an inherent interest and desire to understand where the other is coming from.

7) Stay on topic. It's tempting when we broach an emotional conversation to start unloading all of the things that bother or annoy us about our spouse. Bringing in everything but the kitchen sink to a conversation can move the tone from constructive to destructive quickly.

8) Consider professional help. If you continue to argue rather than discuss your relationship or aspects of your intimacy, and you can't find resolution, consider seeking out a counselor or relationship coach.

Chapter Questions for Real-Life Application

1. Think of a time you've had a successful conversation about a difficult topic? What was the tone and atmosphere? Consider what *you* brought to that conversation that allowed for a positive experience.

2. Is there something you want to talk with your spouse about regarding your intimacy? Are there barriers?

3. Brush up on your listening skills. Ask your spouse when he or she has felt most understood by you.

8
FIRST ENCOUNTERS

If you're a true "beginner," or if this is your second or third marriage, there is always a "first" time

PHEW! YOU MADE IT THROUGH THE WEDDING, FOLLOWED BY the hours of shaking hands. The reception is over, the photos have been taken, and the embracing of all the new in-laws is done! You've just checked into your hotel and you realize, upon walking into your room, that there is, truly, only one bed. So you take your mind off that for a moment by unpacking your things and trying to talk about anything but the elephant in the room—that large, empty, and presently unoccupied bed that you are expected to gladly jump into and have the time of your life!

Whose idea was this anyway? Who said this would be easy, natural, wonderful? You think of your Laurel leader saying that this moment is the time that you have been "waiting for" all your life—and become even more anxious! This is the culmination of that waiting, of all that abstinence during your teenage years. It sounded so romantic and good on TV but now it is ominous and scary and looming large. You might even feel tears welling up, but you don't want your spouse to think you are anything but excited. How could this be? Crying on your wedding night? Oh no! That can't be so! How will he react to that? Will he get in the car and call your mom and tell her to come and get you? Will he ever come back? Now what do you do?

We hope this chapter will help guide you through some of the awkwardness. Remember that the awkwardness is part of the overall experience and can be part of the fun, if you let it.

Remember that you are feeling this way because it is real life, not a Hollywood simulation. It is what you are experiencing at the time. Instead of trying to dismiss these thoughts and feelings, go with them, live them, express them with humor and emotion. Talk about what you are feeling. Laugh about it. Cry about it. Share with your spouse what is going on. Remember, through sharing with those we love we get closer, not further apart. By not sharing, we get what? Further apart.

Do you want to start your relationship closer together or more distant? What precedent are you establishing? You can talk this out and end up having a good experience sharing, talking, and maybe even laughing. Perhaps you will end up going out together and buying a milkshake or going on a nice walk—waiting until you are both ready. If this is the case, you have just learned a significant component to real and healthy intimacy. Share, discover, take a break. Do something familiar before you jump into something unfamiliar and scary.

Scott and Denise

Scott and Denise were both too nervous to be naked in front of each other with the lights on, so they turned them off and decided to try taking a shower together. Unfortunately, all that fumbling around in the dark caused the shower curtain to get knocked off and the shower head to turn toward the bathroom floor, causing a small flood before the water could be turned off and the lights turned back on! In order not to have to explain to the hotel staff what had happened, they quickly turned the lights on and started mopping the floor, naked, and laughing through all the awkwardness.

The question is, can you, right from the beginning, be thoughtful about the other person? Wait? Understand? Show patience? Can you show love, instead of just expressing love, and take the necessary time to make the relationship feel relaxed and comfortable instead of a rushed experience? The key is being there for each other not just doing it with each other.

Guys, you can do this. You will learn how to do this for the rest of your lives, so now is the best time to start. Can you show your wife that it is not all about you and your needs right now? Can you allow her to ease into this experience so her first memory is not, "Well, at least I got through that," instead of "We were really in that together, and he really does care about my needs and feelings."

Travis and April

Travis and April did not have a great honeymoon. The first time she saw him naked, April laughed nervously, as she had never seen a naked, excited man before. She didn't mean to laugh, but she was unprepared. Travis, also nervous, felt like a five-year-old boy when April laughed and immediately retorted back with, "Well, I guess you would rather be here with any other man but me. Probably your ex-boyfriend!" April knew she had hurt him but didn't know how to repair things. They both went to separate corners and already felt like marriage failures.

The next morning, while still in bed, Travis began running his hands over April's body. At first she stiffened because she was still nervous and unsure of where things stood from the night before. However, she also realized this was an important moment and relaxed. She allowed Travis to explore around her body and realized just how much she was enjoying the experience. The more she relaxed, the more excited Travis became as he realized she was responding to him—and him alone.

With morning breath, disheveled hair, and uncertainty, their honeymoon took a new turn. It might not have been the way either of them had anticipated, but it was a beginning.

View Your Honeymoon as a Learning Experience

You might be thinking that the experience Travis and April had the first night of their honeymoon was "bad" while the experience they had in the morning was "good." As humans, we like to put our experiences into neat little categories, like good or bad, in order to sort them out. However, we offer a third consideration. Travis and April's experiences were neither good nor bad but simply educational. Both instances taught them something about themselves, each other, and their relationship.

After all, a relationship consists of two people with two different backgrounds, personalities, genders, and sets of expectations, trying to come together to form something new and unique. This doesn't happen overnight or over the course of a one-week trip in Mexico.

Unfortunately, many couples spend years trying to undo the pain, hurt, or humiliation they experienced during said trip to Mexico. So much emphasis is placed on the honeymoon, and what should or should not happen, that some sort of cataclysmic failure is almost inevitable! Most of the time reality is a lot messier, complex, and satisfying than our "idea" of what we thought it would be like.

Remember, you didn't learn to ride a bike the first time you hopped on. You probably crashed and burned several times, and yet you still got back on. You probably didn't play the piano very well the first time you sat down or could swim across the pool without a lot of lessons and small failures along the way. This new intimate life of yours isn't going to be any different. It's going to be full of ups and downs, hurts and failures, as well as ecstasy and satisfaction. This is something you get to learn and experience together. Don't let one or two moments of misunderstanding, impatience, anxiety, or all-out crashing and burning determine the rest of your married intimate life!

More often than not, we are pretty young, naive, and inexperienced when we walk into that hotel room. Until that moment, you have had a lifetime of trying to learn new things and failing along the way—starting with learning to walk. You already know how to overcome challenges and continue forward. Isn't it wonderful that God lets us learn to fail, get up and try again, fail again, get up and try again, and so on before we ever get married and have to try doing that with another person?

Sexual intimacy is no different! It's hard work from the beginning and will continue to be that way your entire married existence. Remember, it's a mountain landscape and not just a pre-fabricated form. It's a mountain landscape that you two, together, will create. You have the power to decide what you will keep and what you will not—to decide what works and what doesn't. You also have the right as a couple to have a figurative "earthquake" tearing down what you initially started with and begin again. God will help you in this process as He is the Master Creator of all things—including marital intimacy.

In the end, you may find you cherish those moments of "failure" as they propelled you into creating something more rich and beautiful than you could have ever imagined.

REAL RELATIONSHIP TIP!
Keep Your Sense of Humor Intact

This is how David and Loralee described their "first encounter":

"On the first night of our honeymoon while I was 'slipping into something more comfortable' in the bathroom, David decided he would hurry and do push-ups so his muscles would look bigger. Well, he did about forty-five push-ups in thirty seconds and when he stood up, he almost fainted. He lay down on the bed and felt like things were going black!

"So, I come out of the bathroom and he is just lying on the bed without moving a muscle. He whispers, 'You look really good,' but I could tell he was having a hard time talking, so I went over to him and asked him if he was okay. He was trying to hide it at first, but then just told me he did all the push-ups to make himself 'hotter' and was about to pass out! David had to recover for quite some time from nearly passing out. So we just talked and laughed, and I think it actually helped in the long run to settle our nerves. I'm so glad he told me the truth right then and there because I was feeling insecure about him not jumping right up to sweep me off my feet or something.

"Later that night, after we had both finally fallen asleep, David's arm brushed me and I somehow incorporated it into a dream that there was a huge python in the bed, and I jumped up on the bed screaming and tearing at the sheets saying, 'Get the snake! There's a snake!' David woke up in a panic and started screaming and it took us a moment to finally realize it was a dream. We laughed, calmed down, and went back to sleep.

"Two hours later (yes there is more and it's now 4:30 a.m.), we were jolted out of bed again by the sound of the fire alarm! We didn't know what to do! My friend told me of a time when she was staying in a hotel and they evacuated the entire building and some people just had towels wrapped around them for two hours before they could go back inside. I thought of this and told David, 'We've got to get dressed! Quick!'

We were both scrambling around the room looking for clothes and I thought, 'I could either put on this lingerie or my wedding dress! What do I do?' Just then we got a call from the front desk asking if there was a fire in our room, or if we had been lighting candles. David told me to tell them, 'Oh yeah baby, there's a fire in our room . . . *wink, wink*' Well, there wasn't a real fire or anything, and soon the alarm turned off and we all could go back to bed.

"Needless to say, with the nightmare scare and fire alarm on top of everything else, we didn't get much sleep that night. In the morning, David saw a notebook on the nightstand where previous guests of the bed-and-breakfast had written little notes about their stay. David wrote about our crazy night, how we just enjoyed each other, really taking our time. I was so impressed with how sweet and sensitive David was and how concerned he was with not hurting me. It wasn't the passionate scene from Hollywood—but more like a science project—and very sweet and loving. I really do think David set a precedent of being open and honest about things by telling me about the push-ups. I'm glad he wasn't too macho to admit it, even though he was doing it to look more macho. David still comes in after a workout to show me how big his muscles look. I'm a very lucky woman."

If It's Your "First Encounter" but Not Your First Marriage

With the divorce rate what it is, some of you may be getting ready to enter a second or third marriage. In addition, some readers will be re-marrying after a spouse's death. Most of what is written above still applies to you. While you may have a better understanding of how sex works, you have never been intimate with this person. This is still your "first encounter" with each other. You still have to walk into that "hotel room" and be vulnerable, nervous, excited, and so on.

However, you have the added complexity of having a sexual history with another person. No matter how hard you try, your brain will conjure up images and feelings of that person as your brain is trying to make sense of this new experience. It will be looking to compare this moment with other moments in order to process what is happening. If you had a bad or painful experience, you will probably be somewhat anxious. If you had a great experience, you will probably be hoping for the same. It will be your added challenge to try and set those thoughts and feelings aside and be present with your new spouse. There will still be a learning curve and adjustment time as you learn about each other. There will probably even be some mistakes and embarrassing moments. Humor will be your friend.

Be sure to spend some time in our Creating the Conversation chapter and our Sexual History chapter because they contain information that will be so beneficial in helping you transition into this new and exciting chapter of your life.

THE NUTS AND BOLTS

After enduring weeks or months of ribbing concerning your "big night," it's finally here. Now, it's just the two of you driving in nervous silence to the hotel.

The question is, can you, right from the beginning, be thoughtful about the other person? Wait? Understand? Show patience? Can you show love, instead of just express love, and take the necessary time to make the relationship feel relaxed and comfortable—instead of a rushed experience? The key is being there for each other, not just doing it with each other. You are human beings, not just human doings.

Men and women view sex differently—as they do almost everything else. Period. Unfortunately, many couples spend years trying to undo the pain, hurt, or humiliation they experienced during their honeymoon. So much emphasis is placed on what should or should not happen, that some sort of cataclysmic failure is almost inevitable! Most of the time reality is a lot messier, complex, and satisfying than our "idea" of what we thought it would be.

You didn't learn to ride a bike the first time you hopped on. You probably crashed and burned several times, yet you still got back on. You probably didn't play the piano very well the first time you sat down or could swim across the pool without a lot of lessons and small failures along the way. This new intimate life of yours isn't going to be any easier. This is something you get to learn and experience together. Don't let one or two moments of misunderstanding, impatience, anxiety, or all-out crashing and burning determine the rest of your married intimate life!

It's hard—but fun—work from the beginning and will continue to be that way your entire married existence. Remember, it's a mountain landscape and not a pre-fabricated form. It's a mountain landscape you two, together, will create. You have the power to decide what you will keep and what you will not—to decide what works and what doesn't. You also have the right, as a couple, to have a figurative "earthquake" and tear down what you initially started with and start again. God will help you in this process as He is the Master Creator of all things— including marital intimacy. In the end, you may find you cherish those moments of "failure" as they propelled you into creating something more rich and beautiful than you could have ever imagined.

Chapter Questions for Real-Life Application

1. If you're engaged, spend some time discussing any concerns or fears you may have surrounding your upcoming honeymoon. For example, is it imperative for you to have sex the first night? Are there other areas in which you could educate yourself to feel more prepared for your honeymoon?

2. If you've already had a honeymoon, is there anything you haven't resolved that may be getting in the way of your intimacy?

3. Looking back to your honeymoon, what are some things you learned about yourself, your spouse, and your relationship? What has changed since then?

4. What new thing did you learn about what your spouse may like from the chapter?

9

HIS APPROACH,
HER APPROACH

*How the differences in our brains cause us to
approach relationships drastically differently*

EN AND WOMEN ARE DIFFERENT! WE ARE DIFFERENT PHYS-
ically, chemically, and hormonally. These differences
present themselves in a variety of ways, and you may be
wondering what you got yourself into marrying someone from an
entirely different species! However, differences aside, there are a large
amount of similarities: we want to love and be loved, to be understood
and accepted, to feel safe and secure, to have fun, to be spiritual, and
to have meaningful relationships that fosters our ability to grow. At the
core, men and women aren't far apart concerning needs and wants; the
difference lies in the way we approach our needs and wants.

These differences affect the way men approach relationship,
conversation, sex, work, and so on, and they can seem both confusing
and inspiring to women. Conversely, the way a woman approaches
work, friendships, affection, parenting, and so on can seem both inef-
ficient and wonderful. Neither way is wrong, better, or easier than the
other—just different. Once you better understand these differences,
and how they bring a necessary balance to your relationship, we hope
you will better appreciate the great qualities your spouse has and learn
to use these differences to strengthen your relationship.

Scott and Mariah

After they were married, Scott and Mariah were packing the U-Haul to move across the country. Mariah decided she would get things started by packing the truck while Scott was bringing out boxes. When Scott came outside, Mariah smiled at him thinking he would smile back seeing how much she did. Instead, he frowned, put down the boxes he was carrying and began rearranging things Mariah considered to be "packed and done." When she questioned his actions, he said he could tell there wasn't enough room for the boxes he just brought out and he needed to re-pack what she had done. Mariah felt embarrassed, stupid, and a little angry that her hard work had gone unnoticed and unappreciated. She told Scott he could "go ahead and finish packing" without her! Scott wasn't sure how to respond. He wasn't trying to make her mad, but he could see that the boxes simply wouldn't fit in the truck. In confusion, Scott watched her walk away but then turned back to the task at hand, deciding he would figure it out later.

This scenario plays out in a variety of ways between men and women. We could plug in almost any setting—the bedroom, the car, taking a walk—and witness the same type of conversation and outcome. Both Mariah and Scott had the same goal—to pack the U-Haul and be on their way. They both wanted to help the other and share in this task. The underlying want was the same; the difference appeared in the approach. Had Mariah and Scott better understood the way each was wired, perhaps their "first fight" could have waited until they were on the road and needing directions.

Some Fun Brain Differences

In the beginning, boy and girl brains are not that different. Research shows that the brain starts to develop upon conception and evolves through adulthood. However, once it was decided whether or not your brain was male of female, some amazing things occurred: for example, a male brain has a lot more gray matter than a female brain—while a female brain has more white matter.

In a male brain, gray matter is grouped into "information processing centers." This allows it to compartmentalize thoughts, tasks, work, and relationships. The male brain will literally move from one center to the next. Again, notice how Scott was completely focused on packing the U-Haul and remained focused after Mariah walked away.

In a female brain, white matter is spread throughout, allowing different areas to be connected. This structure allows a female to integrate various experiences and continue to gather information quickly and efficiently. Mariah knew Scott wanted to get on the road and that he was also tired and hungry. Noticing this, she sped up the packing process to display her concern for him. She had taken the information and was using it to further her "connection" with him.

Dr. Caroline Leaf, in her book, *Who Switched off Your Brain?*, compares these two structures to "supercomputers" and the "Internet"—with the supercomputers being the areas of gray matter within the male brain and the Internet being like the white matter. Alone, those two structures function fine, but together, they are fantastic! Think of what can be accomplished when these two brains decide to work together. And remember, neither is superior—just different. By embracing these differences, we can become something "more" together than what we are apart.

Referring to our "how sex is like dining" analogy, men and women approach a restaurant and dining experiences uniquely. When going to a restaurant, he will first decide where he wants to go to. Next, he will look at the menu and decide what he wants to eat. Then he will eat his meal until satisfied. She, on the other hand, needs to think about which restaurant she wants to go to and compare her thoughts to other past experiences. Once she decides on a restaurant, she needs to look over every choice on the menu—going back and forth before finally deciding. While she is eating, she will notice the smell and sounds of the restaurant and wonder if her outfit fits in with the decor. After finishing her meal, she will compare her experience to decide if she wants to eat there again. She will also wonder what her spouse thought of the restaurant and if he wants to eat there again.

We aren't trying to oversimplify the male response to the restaurant or suggest that women don't know what they want, when they want it, and how they want it; we're trying to illustrate how a male brain will see a problem or task at hand—choosing a restaurant—figure out a solution, and take action, freeing him up to move to the next task or area of concern. Her brain is integrating the entire experience—trying to make connections and gather information as she goes along. Both approaches, when understood, can help create a mutually satisfying experience.

It's important to understand that men and women experience sight, sound, touch, and information in profoundly different ways. These variations will impact how he will respond to your touch, how she will experience her environment, how he will taste his food, and how she will see the situation and visa versa.

It's important to learn about and understand the way your spouse views sex and intimacy according to their male or female brain and hormones because they are dramatically different. Let's start with the ladies.

A Woman as an Air Traffic Controller

A woman's brain is more integrated—able to multitask and gather information—than a man's. This brain structure is helpful if you are trying to manage the emotions, physical needs, and social nuances around you. It's much harder for a woman to compartmentalize her life because the categories seem to blend together and affect each other. Think of a woman's brain as that of an air traffic controller. She is constantly aware of what all the little "blips" are doing and is making plans for each one at all times. That being said, sex is more than just sex for a woman. A woman may express sexually the happiness she felt as she watched her husband take the garbage out and tuck the kids into bed. The sex "blip" may be going around the screen, but whether or not it reaches its destination safely depends heavily on the experiences of her day with others and with her spouse.

A woman approaches intimacy similarly. For her, all connections must be in place before she can truly be physically intimate with you. If she has had a difficult day at work, burned dinner, or had an argument with you earlier, she will be thinking of all these things. She may seek physical comfort from you through hugging, stroking, or cuddling. Because women don't necessarily need to orgasm in order to have a fulfilling physical experience, your wife is not going to approach all physical encounters with the end-goal of having sex. For her, the feelings of "connection" and "love" she experiences through talking, handholding, and cuddling on the couch can be enough.

You can help her move to a place of desiring physical intimacy by listening and talking through her experiences of the day. This helps her move more into a relaxed state, allowing her to lay these thoughts and concerns aside momentarily.

Again, her approach to emotional, mental, and spiritual intimacy will be much the same. She is looking for "connection." Remember, her brain is wired for integration. Therefore, she is looking to be "integrated" with you. She wants to find connection points through conversation and experiences. In her brain, all things are connected. What happened between the two of you earlier will affect what happens between the two of you later. Due to the connected nature of her brain, she will bring the argument you had two days ago into your current conversation unless it is separately dealt with.

So, if you men are wondering how to more effectively get her to be intimate with you, here are a few tips:

1) For a lot of women, talking *is* foreplay. If she feels listened to and that you are interested in her thoughts, she will be more likely to want to be close physically as well.

2) Don't assume that just because you would like her to grab your crotch as she walks by that she would like the same. Again, remember the relationship piece. Sure, sometimes it's fun and playful to do a quick feel as you're passing each other, but women want to be thought of as more than just breasts and a vagina.

3) Be willing to take some time. It often takes women much longer to orgasm than a man due to the different physical structure of a woman. A man has to ejaculate in order to release semen. Nature has tied ejaculation and orgasm together for a man. A woman doesn't have to achieve orgasm in order to be able to create offspring. Therefore, for a woman, reaching climax is an added bonus that definitely enhances her experience. Being willing to help her get there will help her feel like you see her needs as important.

4) Not every woman needs to have an orgasm every time she has sex in order to feel sexually satisfied. This seems to be a really difficult concept for most men to understand due to the fact that, for men, orgasm *is* the point of sex. This is not necessarily so for a lot of women.

A woman can feel satisfied and close to her husband simply through enjoying sex with him. Additionally, semen is filled with chemicals that are absorbed into the woman's body and helps lift her mood. Sometimes the pressure of feeling that she has to have an orgasm every time she has sex is just too much. Simply asking her, or letting her direct you, will let you know her sexual need at the time.

5) Foreplay is important. For most women, there needs to be some sort of transition time between going to work, making dinner, paying bills, or whatever else is going on, and being intimate. Husbands will have much greater success if they will turn the lights down, rub her shoulders or legs, make sure the door is locked so kids stay out, and so on. Like Dan Gray says in *Men Are from Mars and Women Are from Venus*, women are like crock pots and need time to warm up before the meal is ready to go.

6) Be clean. Women are more attuned, due to the integrated brain, to smells and sights. If you need to shower, do so. Brush your teeth and remove your sweaty socks from the floor beside your bed. A clean man is definitely more of a turn on!

Men as Bowlers

A man's brain is not as integrated—it uses one side at a time. This allows a man to be more focused on a single direction or outcome. Think back to primitive man. The males were the hunters with a single goal—to provide food—period. Their brain allowed them to focus on this task and not get distracted by whatever beautiful sunset, interesting flower, or new trail to follow. In more modern terms, the man is looking down that bowling lane and focusing on nothing other than hitting those pins. He's not wondering how his butt is looking to those behind him, if the song playing is from the '80s or '70s, or if he's going to look stupid when he throws the ball. Nope, he's just thinking about getting that strike.

Men typically approach physical intimacy from a more pragmatic, compartmentalized place. It doesn't matter if he's had a bad day at work or with the kids. He can put those thoughts aside and focus on being physically intimate with you. For him, oxytocin—the bonding chemical in the brain—is primarily released during ejaculation. However, it can also be released through any sort of touch, like hugging or cuddling. The more affection he receives, as well as intercourse itself, the more bonded he will feel to you. Keep in mind, if he's looking to be intimate with you, he's not thinking about the kids' carpool or if the dog needs food—focuses on what is happening in the moment.

That being said, ladies, here are a few tips to help you understand what your man is looking and hoping for:

1) He hopes—no prays—that you will make physical affection and sex a priority. Too often women move this way down on the list thinking their husband is a "big boy" and can take care of himself. Not so. Men feel much closer to their wives through physical touch and especially lovemaking.

2) They are attracted to your body and may try to touch it! Please understand the "going for the strike" mentality. Yes, there will be plenty of times for shoulder rubs, arm tickling, and cheek-to-cheek dancing, but sometimes a man just wants to touch your breasts, bottom, or genitals in passing. It doesn't mean you have to drop everything and have sex right then, it just means he is enjoying you in a sexual way. Instead of rebuffing it, be glad for the interest.

3) Be an active participant in your lovemaking. Contrary to popular belief, men want a willing and active partner in their bed. If you're having sex mostly out of duty, he will notice and it will affect him. While he'll still get some satisfaction from sex itself, he won't feel the same emotional connection he is looking for. Which brings us to point four.

4) Sex is a way a man connects spiritually and emotionally, as well as physically, with a woman. He wants to be close to you literally and figuratively! Be glad and grateful. You have plenty of your own faults and shortcomings, yet he still wants to seek you out. He will slay dragons for you if you will let him!

5) He wants to be seen as William Wallace (*Braveheart*) in your eyes and not Mr. Rogers. Treat him like a man, and he will act like a man. It's especially important to treat him like a man in bed. Enjoy his rougher skin, his smell, and his strength.

6) Dress up for him just as you do for your girlfriends. Face it, ladies, we sometimes spend more time getting ready for other women than we do for our men! Even though they may not notice you changed the color of your lipstick, they will notice your pretty face, clean skin, and nice smelling hair. It makes a difference.

Men approach emotional, mental, and spiritual intimacy similarly. Your husband wants to strategize, come to conclusions, and focus on the "problem" at hand. He genuinely desires to help you, and he cares about your feelings. When he shares his thoughts with you, you may not receive large amounts of information. He is going to share what he feels is pertinent to the conversation. He's not trying to "keep things" from you; he's actively thinking of the current subject—and nothing else. His focus and ability to problem solve are exceptional. By seeing this as a positive, you will see how he displays his love and concern by trying his best to listen and then figuring out the best way to proceed.

Brenda and Nick

Brenda was busy getting dinner ready and trying to wrangle the kids when Nick walked in the door. Normally Brenda would barely acknowledge Nick because of being preoccupied with dinner preparations, who needed to do what homework, have what bath, what bill needed to be paid, and so on. She assumed Nick understood this. However, Brenda's treatment of Nick was causing quite a bit of tension because Nick felt he was on the bottom of Brenda's priority list—finishing just under the category of "bills needing to be paid."

He expressed his frustration to Brenda during one of their weekly walks. When she tried to explain how many things she was trying to juggle, he quickly offered to take over the bills or help with grocery shopping. At first, Brenda felt he was expressing dissatisfaction with the way she was conducting things. However, then she realized he was simply trying to help "solve" a problem she had expressed. She was able to view this as his way of showing her he cared about her and her needs.

The next time Nick came home, Brenda made the conscious effort to actually walk into the front room, smile, and give him a quick hug before returning to making dinner. This small change had a huge effect on Nick. He felt Brenda was actually happy to see him. Her hug helped him feel "welcomed home" and he was more inclined to jump in and help with the kids or dinner.

Two Brains, Two Approaches, One Goal

As you can see, men and women really aren't that far apart. We all want to love and be loved. Usually we want what is best for each other and our relationship, and we go about our day trying to do things to help and not hinder. We get stuck when we don't understand the fundamental differences in the way men and women approach intimacy and relationship. Ladies, be glad you are married to a man! He will help you solve problems, see situations clearly, and open those jars. Men, be glad you are married to a woman! She will help gather missing information and make connections, and she smells so much better than your buddies.

Spend some time observing how your spouse approaches areas of concern, parenting, work, and chores and notice her ideas. Instead of simply dismissing them or becoming frustrated, see how he is genuinely trying to help, using the very brain God gave him.

THE NUTS AND BOLTS

Here is some information you may or may not be aware of—men and women are different! We are different physically, chemically, and hormonally. These differences present themselves in a variety of ways, and you may wonder sometimes just what the heck you got yourself into marrying someone who seems from an entirely different species! However, casting differences aside, there are an amazing amount of similarities as well.

Men and women want to love and be loved; be understood; learn; feel safe; be compassionate; have fun; be spiritual; and have meaningful, intimate relationships. At our cores, men and women aren't that far apart when it comes to needs and wants—the difference lies in the way we approach our needs and wants.

The variances in approach lie in the ways our brains, chemicals, and hormones are structured. A man's brain is designed to be more compartmentalized and focused. A woman's brain is designed to be more integrative and tangential. Neither of these structures is better; they're simply different. In fact, when working together, these structures are incredible! The key is learning about these differences, learning to appreciate them, and then learning to work with them and not against them.

After reading this chapter, you should have a greater ability to understand the way your spouse approaches physical, emotional, mental, and spiritual intimacy

---

Chapter Questions for Real-Life Application

1. What is something new you learned about the opposite sex? Discuss this with each other, demonstrating greater understanding for the way you communicate.

2. Think about your last sexual experience with each other. Is there something you could do to enhance the next experience now that you understand better how your spouse approaches physical intimacy?

3. Either look at or think about your spouse and list five great things you like about being married to someone with such a "different" approach. Basically, ladies, list what you like about men, and men, list what you like about women. See how your lists compare.

10
SEXUAL NORMALCY

*Defining your own sexual norms in your relation-
ship and throwing out the Hollywood messages*

T HERE ARE A LOT THINGS IN LIFE THAT HAVE ACCEPTABLE
norms such as your cholesterol levels, tire pressure, and college
entrance exams. Believe it or not, there really isn't a set of
acceptable norms when it comes to your level of intimacy with your
spouse. While the media, your well-meaning friends, and family may
try to give you their opinion of what they consider to be "normal," we
give you permission to just let what they say slide right off your back.
Your relationship with your spouse, and what is healthy and works
well, is your "norm." Since life is about change, your "normal" changes
with age, circumstance, well-being, health, and desire.

A Quick Word of Caution

These standards apply to couples where one or both do not have
mental health concerns such as personality disorders or being raised
in sexually abusive or incestuous homes or by highly dysfunctional
parents. In order to be functionally healthy, we must have learned functional boundaries in our youth and have the skills to apply them in our
own relationships. Individuals who were not blessed to be reared by
boundaried parents, and who come from dysfunctional homes, often

manifest the same dysfunctions in their adult relationships. Learning these boundaries provides us and our children capacities and functions that children from abusive homes don't learn. Nor do they have the ability to create these safeguards in their marriages by themselves. Do not expect an individual from these dysfunctional backgrounds to establish healthy sexual boundaries in their relationship. They may try to convince you they have the capacity, but in reality they do not. In other words, if you've never tasted an orange, how could you describe the flavor to someone else? The same holds true with relationships: if you never experienced a healthy and boundaried relationship, it will be difficult to know how to create one. If you are in a marriage with someone with this background, or if you have this background, please know that extra work, patience, forgiveness, compassion, and humility will be required. Additionally, it would be wise to seek out professional help to learn how to develop a healthy, boundaried marriage.

Your Relationship Is as Unique as a Snowflake

Often the media will report on some new finding or study about how often couples are having sex or how satisfied people are with their sex lives. They'll attempt to put some sort of quantitative number to something incredibly individual and specific. Any statistician will tell you that you have to look beyond the reported numbers, who was asking the questions, what the questions were, and to whom they were being asked—not to mention who was funding the study to begin with. Numbers, and the interpretation thereof, are often misrepresented.

While these types of studies help to create a baseline for therapists and other professionals, they should not be used to define your relationship or view your spouse. Just as no two snowflakes are identical, no two marital relationships are exactly alike either!

Look around your book club, bowling league, church group, or whatever group you are in. You are all there because you share a similar interest and therefore you probably have some similarities in your likes and personalities. However, if you look even one figurative centimeter deeper, most perceived similarities diverge. Your relationship, complete with the individual aspects of your personality and your spouse's, will look incredibly different from anyone around you. Therefore, your sexual relationship and how you respond to one another intimately will be drastically different.

Getting Past the Distorted Messages from Hollywood

According to multiple marketing-research studies, we are exposed to over three thousand messages a day. How many of these have sexual content of some sort? If we are getting our lessons in love and sex from Hollywood, there will be a lot of disappointment, confusion, resentment, and an unhealthy striving to fit our sex life into an unrealistic box.

Flip on any TV, walk past a newsstand, or browse the Internet, and you're going to see an ad, video clip, or picture depicting what "your" sexual life could and should be if only you . . . wore a certain perfume, drank a certain beverage, had a certain body, or drove a certain car. One thing advertisers know is that sex sells, and it sells big. Sex and intimacy are depicted in all forms and varieties throughout the media—usually in a distorted fashion. We are constantly bombarded with messages we are required to sort through and decide what we are going to internalize and what we are going to throw out. For the most part, just throw it all out.

Do you have a tendency to believe what you see in these images more than what you feel in everyday life? Do you trust what is real in your everyday experience and compare your reality with the myths being shoved your way? Do you question if these images are real? Are they depicting what you know, feel, or experience? Do people sweat in these images? Do they have bad breath? Do they have to go to work? Pay bills? Use the toilet? Consider STDs or pregnancy? Work out relationship differences? Go get a crying baby? Have periods? Pass gas? And just generally be human?

Our everyday experiences are not Hollywood's definition of glamorous or sexy, but they are real and vibrant. Ads, movies, and TV showcase the ideal wife or husband doing all of the things our spouses *aren't* doing, and suddenly we find ourselves comparing our spouses' weaknesses against an edited Hollywood person's finest attributes. They don't stand a chance!

If we were following Hollywood's rules, couples would be having orgasmic sex every time they were having sex. Beds would be breaking.

They would be having sex at least 3.2 times a week. Women would be slender, despite having children, and wouldn't have stretch marks or extra weight. The men would all be handsome and muscular and would be romancing the women with flowers, compliments, and spontaneous dates; they would be the perfect husband.

We can get caught up in these scenarios when we are unhappy, disappointed, looking for a quick-blame fix, or when we get lazy and tired in our relationships and no longer want to do the necessary work to correct the errors in our thinking or the reality of myths. In other words, we are not always up to the work that is required to achieve good marriages and to experience sex that is fulfilling. We bring these myths into our relationship and use them unjustly to compare them to our own relationship. Hollywood wants us to stay in our dysfunctional part of our brains where we do not think clearly—where we blame and are highly critical. Where we tend to believe there is someone who wants exactly what we want, thinks exactly as we think, and will love us exactly how we want to be loved, even though we are humanly flawed.

Hollywood, social media, and blogs would have you believe that people are living incredible lives filled with all of the intimacy and romance you could ever want, while you are sitting at home missing out. We are here to tell you this is simply not true. We watch movies, read books, and watch TV in order to check out of reality for awhile and relax. The key phrase in that sentence is "check out." Reality is messy, ever-changing, passionate, tiring, and full of ups and downs. By accepting reality and acknowledging the unreality of the media around us, we will be able to forgive ourselves and our spouse for being what we are—human.

Hit the Buffet Line and Enjoy Some Variety

The format of this book is not a "how to" when it comes to sex. It's a book designed to help you gain a better understanding of yourself, your partner, your relationship, and the intimacy found therein. That being said, variety is a good thing. There are about twenty thousand species of butterflies in the world! Everywhere you look in nature, you can find something different. Trees, grasses, and landscapes are different. Remember, your relationship is as rich and varied as a mountain landscape as opposed to neat, symmetrical triangles.

As human beings, we enjoy experiencing new things. We enjoy finding out if we like something, or if we think it's bland, gross, ugly, and so on. To use our food analogy, most of us enjoy eating a variety of food.

This book isn't going to give you a list of different sexual positions or the names of appropriate lingerie shops. There are some fantastic resources already available. What we will try and reinforce is the intimate and personal nature of *your* relationship. Do you want to try a new position? Do you like lingerie? What type of lingerie? Do you always have to have sex in the bedroom with the lights off, or could sex on the couch be acceptable? What about in the shower? Every individual is sexually different. There is no "one size fits all" when it comes to sexual tastes, desires, fantasies, turn-ons, and so on. Therefore, your two main friends will be communication and experimentation.

Scott and Danielle

Scott's job allowed him to come home for lunch a couple of times a week. One time Danielle surprised him by meeting him at the door, scantily clothed. Scott immediately understood Danielle's intentions and they enjoyed an intimate moment right in the front room—with curtains closed and front door locked, of course. Scott later remarked to Danielle how great that was and how he went back to work feeling fantastic—not just because they had had sex, but because it was something out of their ordinary routine.

Frequency

One of the most common questions couples ask is how often other couples are having sex. Again, it's nice to have some sort of baseline to give context to your experience, but it's all relative. According to the Kinsey Institute, 47 percent of couples are having intercourse an average of one time per week. But that's an average that will vary markedly over a lifetime. You will inevitably face relationship circumstances (such as the addition of children, new job, death of a family member), medical circumstances, as well as other stressors. Couples have periods when they are not having sex at all or times when they're having more sex than their usual. A baseline can be helpful to see where you fall on the spectrum and to see if you would like to adjust your frequency in either direction. Again, the premise of this chapter is to give you usable information that can help you find your "normal," learn to communicate as a couple, and trust your experience.

A Few Other Dishes on the Sexual Buffet Table

There seems to be a need within us to feel we are "okay" and doing things like other people. We sometimes like to feel that we are all eating at the same buffet line, using our "how sex is like dining" analogy again. There is something comforting about showing up to a ward party and seeing the typical fare—funeral potatoes, sliced ham, and basketball hoops. So how do we go about defining some typical aspects of sexual relationships without creating new sets of "normal boundaries"? It's tough, but let's refer to our buffet line:

Imagine you're at your ward party. The prayer has been said, and the crowd heads to the food. Although the people, location, and food are generally the same, there are subtle variations. There might be turkey instead of ham, several kinds of funeral potatoes, and punch as well as water. As you're going through the line, some people may skip the meat and head for the salad and potatoes. Perhaps you decide you are not that hungry and have a little dessert! As you can see, once you start thinking about it, you can have quite the variety within a seemingly typical occasion. This is the same for our intimate life.

There is a quote from a handbook produced by the LDS Church that advises people to guard against anything "unnatural" within the bonds of their sexual relationship. This is where semantics come into play. What exactly does "unnatural" mean? Is it "unnatural" to stick your tongue in your spouse's ear because the ear isn't a "natural" place for a tongue to go? Some people interpret "unnatural" to mean anything other than the traditional missionary sexual position, while others have a much broader definition of the word. Who is right?

We view the topic of sexual normalcy as important for a couple to discuss and decide what works for them and enhances their relationship. What you and your spouse feel comfortable with is within the realm of your stewardship over your marriage. Over and over couples are counseled to decide for themselves what will happen in their sexual relationship and what will not. The important thing is to openly communicate about what you're comfortable with as well as what you would like to explore and what you would not. It must not be in the spirit of coercion, force, or abuse. You must include the Lord and the Spirit in these decisions. Remember those Doctrine and Covenants suggestions to, "let virtue garnish thy thoughts unceasingly; then shall thy confidence wax strong." (Doctrine and Covenants 121:45)

For some basic definitions, health considerations, and an ongoing discussion about the topics like vibrators, oral sex, masturbation within marriage, and anal sex, visit our website:

www.RealIntimacyBook.com or www.TheHealingGroup.com.

You, Your Spouse, and God Are the Stewards of This Relationship

Elder James E. Faust said, "The prophets, seers, and revelators have had and still have the responsibility and privilege of receiving and declaring the word of God for the world. Individual members, parents, and leaders have the right to receive revelation for their own responsibility but have no duty nor right to declare the word of God beyond the limits of their own responsibility."

We should never control another in any relationship—especially sexual. We must show kindness and pure knowledge. Not just what we think it means or how we think the other person feels, but it must be pure knowledge. We cannot receive this through supposition, speculation, or telling her what she believes. We must, through patience and long-suffering, truly come to know and understand ourselves, spouse, and relationship—which does not mean a few minutes or hours or even weeks of waiting. We must decide if we are willing to wait it out long enough until we come to the truth and sincerely wait upon the other person, to let her have the time and energy to figure it out in her own mind and to come to an understanding of how she really feels, and how that feeling can then be put into action. This is done through kindness, which greatly enlarges the soul—your soul and his soul—as well as gentle persuasion, without being phony, cheeky, rude, or critical. Then things can then work together for your good, and you can then start to come together in love and affection—finding your sexual norm.

THE NUTS AND BOLTS

What is normal? It seems to be something we all strive to achieve, but who gets to decide if we're normal or not? Do we allow outside forces and influences to determine our normalcy, or do we discover for ourselves what is normal for us? Helping you discover and talk about what is normal and "okay" for your relationship was the goal of this chapter.

We are constantly bombarded by messages from the media, Internet, colleagues, friends, teachers, and family about what "should" or "should not" occur within our personal, private marital relationship. Our advice is to throw out most of what you are hearing. Is it fair to compare your relationship to one depicted in a two-hour, edited, and air-brushed movie? Or to compare your relationship to Brother and Sister So-and-So as they gush at each other over the pulpit? Just as you don't understand the nuances of their relationship, it's not fair to compare yours to the tiny picture presented by others or the media. Most people only display the "tip of the iceberg" when it comes to themselves or their relationship.

There are several topics that are usually considered taboo, but are nonetheless prevalent in many marital relationships and in the media, and are therefore worth discussing. For information about topics like vibrators, oral sex, masturbation within marriage, and anal sex, visit our website for a current forum and ongoing discussion: www .RealIntimacyBook.com or www.TheHealingGroup.com.

There is a quote from a handbook produced by the Church that advises people to guard against anything "unnatural" within the bonds of their sexual relationship. This is where semantics come into play. What exactly does "unnatural" mean? Is it "unnatural" to stick your tongue in your spouse's ear because the ear isn't a "natural" place for a tongue to go? Some people interpret "unnatural" to mean anything other than the traditional missionary sexual position, while others have a much broader definition of the word. Who is right?

Couples are counseled to decide for themselves what will happen in their sexual relationship—and what will not. The important thing is to openly communicate about what you're comfortable with and what you would like to explore. It must not be in the spirit of coercion, force, or abuse. It's important to include the Lord and the Spirit in these decisions.

Chapter Questions for Real-Life Application

1. Define your "norm" with your spouse. Is your norm to have sex 3–4 times a week, 3–4 times a month, or 3–4 times a year? Has that always been consistent, or has that changed with circumstances?

2. Is there anything you would like to add to your sexual dining experience? Discuss this with your spouse and be open to their response and reaction. This is more about learning to open the door to communication. If he is not interested in "sampling" the dish you are requesting, keep in mind how you would respond if they didn't want to share in a new flavor of popcorn you wanted to try.

3. Is there anything you would like to remove from your sexual dining experience that you haven't talked about?

4. How much have Hollywood, the literature you read, or your friends and family influenced your personal feelings concerning the validity of your marital relationship? Take an inventory of the negative feelings you may be harboring and throw them out!

11
UNDERSTANDING YOUR LIBIDO

How this little word greatly affects
your sexual dining experience

WHAT IN THE WORLD IS YOUR "LIBIDO"? THIS WORD SEEMS to be something kicked around a lot in conversation without anyone truly knowing what it means. Everyone gives the knowing nod and subtly tries to change the subject in order not to give themselves away. The word "libido" could be substituted for the phrase "sex drive." Does that help? So, if we're trying to understand our sex-drive or our spouse's, we usually focus on whether it is "high" or "low" and that's about it. Like everything else we've discussed, your libido, or sex drive, isn't an either/or status. It can, and does, change constantly due to several factors that we will discuss in this chapter. You will come to see how breaking down libido will improve your ability to understand yourself and your spouse—which will serve to enhance your intimacy overall.

Kristi and Steve

Kristi would listen to her girlfriends talk about how their husbands just seemed to want sex all the time and she tried to make sense of what was happening in her marriage. She wondered if her friends were exaggerating, or if their husbands really did want to be intimate as often as they were saying. She and Steve, it seemed, hardly had sex at all. In fact, not only were they not having sex, but Steve just didn't seem interested in being affectionate either. After asking him if he was having an affair and being told no, Kristi expressed concern about their sex life. Steve admitted he just wasn't that interested in sex and knew he "should" be—being a man—which only made him feel worse. He had just decided to avoid the situation altogether, including being affectionate at all with Kristi.

They decided to investigate what could be happening. Both started with the assumption that nothing was "wrong" with Steve, but that maybe there was something they were missing. During a counseling session, the counselor asked Steve if he was taking any sort of medication. Steve said he was taking anti-depressants for ongoing depression. The counselor nodded his head and began to explain how certain medications can affect a person's sex drive and that there were things that could be done to help alleviate some of those side effects.

Kristi and Steve knew there was going to be more work ahead, but they were glad to at least understand what they were working with. Also, having that information helped Kristi to be much more patient and understanding, as she encouraged Steve to make a more conscious effort to reach out to her physically.

What Makes Up Sex Drive?

Obviously there is a lot more gray area than you may have imagined. As you probably noticed, this book employs a lot of gray boxes filled with helpful information. When you work in the field of "people," your favorite color soon becomes gray. With a few exceptions, most issues contain a lot of variables—remember that mountain landscape or the sexual buffet table. Let's break down the three main components that make up your sex drive:

1) Sexual Capacity: Your capacity is your physical ability to become sexually aroused and have an orgasm. Your overall physical health, including your muscular and nervous systems, affect your sexual capacity. Our sexual capacity varies throughout life as we grow, develop, and learn more about our bodies non-sexually and sexually. Your sexual capacity will greatly change from when you are young to a mature adult.

2) Sexual Motivation: Your sexual motivation, or desire, is what you feel like doing sexually. We are not talking about "positions" necessarily, but your desire to be intimate with your partner. Hormones—such as testosterone and estrogen—learning experiences, religion, or special circumstances will all have an influence on your motivation. Sexual motivation is mostly affected by psychological factors such as stress, relational strain, anxiety surrounding your body image, sexual abuse, and so on. Again, sexual motivation is going to vary from person to person as well as at different times through the life span.

3) Sexual Performance: Sexual performance is looking at the objective amount of sexual activity you are having (not how much of a sexual star you are). Think of this as if you were having a conversation with your spouse about your sexual activity or "performance," such as the number of times you have sex in a week. Sexual performance is going to be affected by both sexual motivation and sexual capacity. For example, if you are not married and are honoring the standards of your religion, you won't be acting on your motivation though you're perfectly capable. Obviously this will affect your performance (sexual outcomes).

The HWH Sexual Libido Spectrum (Hodson, Worthington, Harrison)

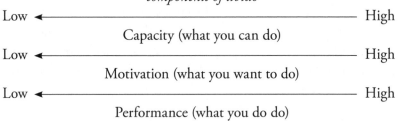

Model created from Dickenson, Kinsey, and Kirkland research on components of libido

Low ◄——————————————————— High
Capacity (what you can do)

Low ◄——————————————————— High
Motivation (what you want to do)

Low ◄——————————————————— High
Performance (what you do do)

Look at each of the spectrums and consider where you fall in each of the areas. Maybe you have the ability to be turned on and can experience an orgasm, but you and your partner have been fighting. You haven't felt like being intimate, which in turn has affected your sexual performance or your amount of sexual activity.

Another potential scenario may be that you are high on the performance scale but are not necessarily aroused nor experiencing an orgasm, although you have high motivation. Could there be a medical circumstance such as a medication that affects your ability to sustain erections? Could the medication inhibit production of natural lubrication, creating pain? Is there a life circumstance, such as ill health, that is limiting your capacity to reach an orgasm or have sex at all?

Using the Diagram as a Learning Tool

Since this book is about your relationship, and not just your individual libido, just how often do you think you and your spouse are going to line up perfectly on the above diagram? Perhaps the main reason you are reading this book is the feeling of being completely out of sync with your spouse most of the time! It would be helpful for you and your spouse to discuss where you both feel you are on the spectrums and where you would like to be. You may be surprised by where you actually are versus where you think you and your spouse think you are.

Understanding the components to your "sex drive" may help you understand yourself and your spouse far better when it comes to your desire for intimacy. Often when we talk about someone's sex drive we are only referencing one aspect of this very complicated concept, which is far more than just examining a person's sexual motivation or desire. However, research shows that a sex drive has more components to it than simply desire, but it's desire gets the blame when intimacy is strained in a relationship. Ideally, understanding where you both are on the spectrum will create room for the expansion and contraction of your sexual relationship and identify where you are, were, and would like to be, while also giving you both greater understanding as to where there are potential sex drive mismatches in your relationship.

Breaking the libido down into components may take some tension out of the conversation, allowing for more meaningful insight into one another. For example, if you understood that your spouse was feeling completely overwhelmed by kids and work and was just trying to survive, therefore lowering her "motivation," would that allow you to see the situation in a new light instead of thinking she "wanted nothing to do with me?" It allows you to remove yourself from the situation and gain a clearer perspective on yourself, your spouse, and your relationship.

Understanding Yourself and Your Spouse as Individuals and Not Just a "Typical" Man or Woman

There are many marriages where the typical stereotypes are turned upside down and are often opposite of every social norm. For example, the wife may be the one who has the higher desire and the husband just isn't highly motivated toward sexual activity. To make things even more complicated, sexuality for men and women will inevitably vary significantly throughout life.

Rather than solely looking at sexuality through a stereotypical lens—such as traditional husband and wife—we'd like to approach it from a neutral position. While a large portion of the population experiences sexuality in a similar manner (for example, the wife tends to be low desire and the husband high desire), we want to create room for those outside the norm.

The point is to discover where you and your spouse fall on the spectrums so you can identify differences and problems relative to your relationship. This way you won't evaluate your relationship based on what you think your friends are experiencing or what Hollywood says you should be experiencing. This will not only help you start to feel like your experiences are valid but will also break feelings of isolation.

Sexual Apathy—When You Have "Lost Your Appetite"

On occasion, a spouse experiences sexual apathy, where the motivation is diminished or completely gone, which affects capacity and performance. On her blog, Natasha Helfer Parker addressed the issue of "sexual apathy," or, in other words, when one of you isn't "hungry" at all.

Sexual apathy is a problem that plagues many marriages. It can be a difficult issue to address, mainly because the nature of the problem is the problem: lack of desire. There can be underlying issues that account for apathy and indifference, and it is important to know that these issues can often be resolved. When couples disagree over the frequency of sex or the type of sexual encounter that is acceptable, it is paramount that they be willing to begin an open, nonjudgmental, and honest discussion together. It is usually not the case that there is no specific reason for a lack of interest in sexual intimacy. We are all born with a sexual self that is inherent to who we are as children of God. Unfortunately, many things can happen to this sexual self along life's journey that take it off its intended course. Sexual apathy is usually a symptom of deeper—many times hidden or even unconscious—issues.

Rick and Allison

Rick and Allison were stuck. Allison basically wanted nothing to do with sex. After the birth of their third and final child, Allison announced to Rick she would no longer be having sex with him. She said she didn't enjoy it or derive any satisfaction from it. Rick was devastated and felt like he was trapped in a marriage in which his needs were never going to be met. He didn't want to be unfaithful to Allison, but he also didn't feel like he could live in this type of situation. They both expressed a deep love and commitment toward one another and their children but didn't know how to resolve this area of their relationship.

Allison eventually consented to see a medical doctor. After having her thyroid tested, it was determined her thyroid was low, a common occurrence after childbirth, which was affecting her energy and mood levels. Allison began taking supplements to improve the functioning of her thyroid.

Once Allison began to feel physically better, she tearfully revealed to Rick that she had been molested as a young teen. She had never told anyone and had always felt "dirty" as a result. She decided to seek counseling for the emotional implications of that experience.

After looking at the HWH Sexual Spectrum Diagram, Allison and Rick both came to see how Allison's capacity had been diminished by her thyroid problems and her motivation being lowered due to the emotional aftermath of the terrible trauma experienced as a young girl. Obviously, performance would basically be at a zero.

Rick took a step back and realize Allison had more going on than just a "low sex drive" and was able to support her as she began working through her various issues. With time, they were both hopeful their sexual relationship could improve.

Shades of Gray . . .

Your libido is more than high or low, raging or non-existent, male or female. It's continually in flux. Not only is yours changing, but that of your spouse. Where you fit along the spectrum will change according to a variety of factors and circumstances. The important thing is to allow for those changes and learn to recognize them and to not take them personally. There is usually a reasonable explanation that can be dealt with medically, emotionally, or with time and patience.

Every relationship has its own rhythm and pattern. If your sexual differences lie in the area of motivation, revisit our chapter entitled Living Deliberately. Consider seeking professional help if you continue to struggle with motivation, wonder about a potential medical condition, or have identified something painful in your sexual history.

REAL RELATIONSHIP TIP!
Better Sex With Aging

According to marital and intimacy expert Dr. David Schnarch, PhD, the best sexual intimacy comes later in life—during your forties, fifties, and sixties. "We have confused sexual prime with genital prime. If you want intimacy during sex, there isn't a sixteen-year-old that can keep up with a healthy sixty-year-old. People are capable of much better sex and intimacy as they mature." Isn't that great news? As we age, we gain more life experience, have learned more lessons, are more comfortable in our skin, and have increased capacity to bring our authentic selves to the table. If you are experiencing sexual difficulties in your marriage now at a younger age, it's not a concrete indicator this is how your sex life will be for the rest of your lifetime. Our sexuality is continually changing and evolving—which isn't a negative but a positive—and is filled with hope, potential, and a lifetime of enjoyable, sexual phases.

THE NUTS AND BOLTS

What in the world is your "libido"? This word seems to be something kicked around a lot in conversation without anyone truly knowing what it means. Everyone gives the knowing nod and subtly tries to change the subject in order not to give themselves away. The word "libido" could be substituted for the phrase "sex drive." Does that help? So, if we're trying to understand our sex drive or our spouse's, we usually focus on whether it is "high" or "low" and that's about it. Like everything else we've discussed, your libido isn't an either/or status. It can, and does, change constantly due to several factors that we discussed in this chapter. You will come to see how breaking down "libido" will improve your ability to understand yourself and your spouse, which will serve to enhance your intimacy overall.

This chapter breaks down libido into three areas: sexual capacity, sexual motivation, and sexual performance.

1) Capacity is your ability to engage in physical intimacy. Things like health, stress, sleep deprivation, and medication can all affect your capacity. If your spouse is seriously ill, their capacity is basically zero. It has nothing to do with you or their desire but with their ability.

2) Motivation has to do with your feelings concerning physical intimacy. Things like anxiety, resentment, anger, desire, and so on affect your motivation. If you fight and argue constantly, chances are your motivation for sex is going to be low. It has nothing to do with your capacity.

3) Performance has to do with what you are actually doing. Are you having sex or not? It has nothing to do with how "good" at it you are.

It will be important to look at the HWH Sexual Libido diagram presented in this chapter to better understand these three areas and where you and your spouse find yourselves on it. It will be an interesting exercise to see the areas you match and the areas you don't.

You will come to see that "sex drive" has less to do with being a man or a woman, but more to do with your age, health, circumstance, and relationship. These factors are constantly in flux and change almost daily, which affects your overall sexual capacity, motivation and performance.

Breaking it down will allow you to see which area needs tweaking and will give you a clearer sense of direction. Instead of wondering why your spouse's "sex drive" is so low or high compared to yours, you will be able to discern the reason more clearly, giving you something to work with.

Chapter Questions for Real-Life Application

1. Find yourself and your spouse on the capacity, motivation, and performance diagram.

2. Where do you and your spouse match and differ? How can you work with this information to improve your sexual relationship, address concerns, and have greater patience and compassion for your spouse?

3. Did your findings come as a surprise to either you or your spouse?

12

LIVING DELIBERATELY

How to create a satisfying sexual relationship when the "feelings" just aren't there. Sexual intimacy breeds the desire for more sexual intimacy

IKE SEEMED TO HAVE IT RIGHT WHEN IT CREATED THE slogan, "Just Do It!" In the land of consistently changing behaviors, spending time trying to understand "why" you don't have a desire for sex will too frequently not create intimacy in the bedroom, unless you couple that question with action. To put it another way, would understanding why you don't like going to the gym get you to the gym? Not unless you take that understanding and pair it with the action of getting to the gym. The goal of this chapter is to identify strategies and actions for increasing sexual intimacy. If you find you are unable to get out of a rut, there are additional resources in the back of the book that might be useful.

Katie and Dan

After seventeen years of marriage, six children, and working part time, Katie just didn't feel much desire for sex. She didn't know if it was because she was just tired or if there could be other reasons. She found herself sneaking off to bed early in order to avoid any awkwardness with her husband. She knew she should want to have sex, but she couldn't seem to muster the energy to actually follow through. Katie could see how it was affecting her husband Dan but kept putting off any sort of conversation about it, hoping her desire would just magically return or his would somehow just go away.

"Intimacy" as a Verb

When it comes to individuals and couples who come to a professional counseling setting, the reason we most often hear of why they do not change or do what is needed to bring about the changes they seek, is that they simply don't feel like doing what is needed to make the change possible. They just never seem to get around to it. The more they think about the feelings they are feeling or not feeling, the more this thinking seems to reinforce their not doing anything to change the logjam. Your mind attempts to sell the "idea" that maybe you'll feel like doing this, that, or the other, tomorrow or the next day or after getting through this month or after losing this weight. In reality, it actually seems to work just the opposite. What we put off doing never seems to really happen.

If we allowed only our feelings to steer and dictate our course of action, many of us, in the end, end up doing very little. If we persisted in this course of action, too many of us would quit our jobs after a bad week or two, and we would find ourselves going on a ten-day adventure tour of New Zealand on a whim or living far more selfishly. This isn't to say that our feelings don't matter—they make us human, authentic, and able to connect with others. Our duty-bound and task-based selves can become out of balance, resulting in relational and personal dysfunction. Moreover, our emotional side can become out of balance, often resulting in chaos, dysfunction, and action based only on desire. We are creatures of habit and can get into a groove with habits that are counterproductive in our relationships. The more we don't do important things because we don't feel like doing them, the more our relationships will suffer.

The Law of Living Deliberately

Some common examples of this would be church activities, exercise, cleaning the house, drinking water, and in this case, having sex. There is a time and place for both approaches. Both approaches are necessary in a balanced and functional life. We have to be proactive with our life to become what we want—we must live deliberately.,

If a client is stuck in a rut—sexually or otherwise—because of a lack of desire or motivation, we assign them the law of "Living Deliberately." We challenge their comfort zone and help create new traits or qualities that can enhance their lives or improve a relationship.

This rule works counter to the "I don't feel like it" tendency that we experience when the task we face is hard or complicated. The rule is simply this: When you live deliberately, you do nothing based on whether you feel like it or not. You do it because you decided in advance that it was something you wanted to do because it was in your best interest. (If you are having more serious aversions that are more than just a slump or lack of motivation, see our chapter, "When to Seek Professional Help.")

Kelly and Joe

Kelly and Joe have been married for seven years and have two kids. Kelly is a dedicated mother and has a part-time job outside of the home. Joe has a typical nine-to-five job. As they began dating, their chemistry was "explosive," yet they didn't ever become involved in such a way that would have jeopardized their standing with the Church. Their honeymoon night was great for Joe but not as great for Kelly. Over the course of their marriage, the frequency of intimacy slowly waned, and Kelly started to feel more and more anxiety as nighttime came.

She found herself angry that Joe didn't appear to value more of the other aspects of their marriage. Joe's resentment and frustration started to build as their intimacy lessened. Although they talked about their sexual difficulties, Kelly felt Joe should respect the fact that she did not want to have sex. Kelly knew she "should and could" have more sex with her husband but was tired and didn't feel emotionally connected to him. She also had no intention of actively trying to understand her lack of sexual desire within their relationship.

In the above scenario, you may identify with Kelly or Joe— or maybe you can see the side of both individuals in this marriage. Michelle Weiner in her book, *The Sex Starved Marriage*, cites some interesting research about desire. Most of the time we think that desire precedes action—that being "turned on" comes before being intimate. However, research shows that for many people, feeling turned on comes after intimacy has begun. Again, put in a less emotionally charged way, think about the last time you went to the gym when you didn't want to. Didn't it feel good when you were done with your workout? How about once you got on the treadmill, put in your headphones, and got going? If people went to the gym or exercised only when they felt like it, we would have even more lethargic, out-of-shape, and ornery people.

However, once you get to the gym and actually get involved in your workout, it usually becomes easier to exercise. You start enjoying the benefits of exercise and, at the same time, you have improved your health, stamina, technique, and ability. You may not love going to exercise every time. Who does? In fact, you may only be going to the gym because your gym partner is expecting you to show up. And is that such an awful thing? Sure, everyone experiences times when they stop going to the gym for a while, but then, one day, you make the decision to grab your workout stuff and head out the door—whether or not you truly feel like it.

You can do this because you can recall how good it felt to exercise, or you may not like what has happened to your body during your hiatus from the gym. Exercise is a lifetime of committing and recommitting every day. Why? Because it's healthy for us. Sex is the same way. It is also healthy for us and our relationships. It is an element of marriage that connects us to each other in a way that we cannot be connected with anyone else. It is worth the effort and the time. So at times the mantra must be, "just do it!"

Finding Yourself on the Sexual Spectrum

Take the above analogy and apply it toward your marital relationship. You may not have had sex in a while or even been physically affectionate. You may resent having someone counting on you to share this experience. You may have a low desire toward sex in general, and each time there is an intimate experience, it's work. All of these experiences are a part of the sexual spectrum. Like your feelings toward exercise, you may have varying "seasons" where you are more into it than others.

We are not going to pitch the faulty idea that healthy sex a certain number of times a week makes for a healthy marriage. In fact, assigning a numerical value to your intimacy can be extremely counterproductive. We want you to find a place within your marriage that works for you and your partner. You may want to review the chapter on how sex is like dining to understand the whole buffet of experiences. But as a starting point, it may be helpful to schedule intimacy sessions—being it mental, emotional, spiritual, or physical.

Back to our scenario with Joe and Kelly. Joe clearly would like to have more intimate experiences, and Kelly would like to go to bed without feeling like Joe is going to try something. Kelly continues to feel that she doesn't want to have sex and has no desire to work on it. Yet she wants Joe to engage her emotionally, remain faithful, and be a happy husband. We realize the idea of infidelity is taboo in our gospel culture, yet it is more prevalent than we give it credit. We are also not placing the full weight of infidelity on the shoulders of the low desire spouse, but we do want to point out the incongruity of the expectations—"I am not going to have sex with you, yet I want you to remain happy and faithful." This can go both ways in terms of emotional and sexual intimacy. Ultimately we are asking for the same thing.

Imagine if conversation were what helped you feel connected in a relationship and your spouse decided not to speak to you for months at a time. Would you expect her to be happy? At the very least, she might fantasize about what it would be like talking with someone else. Let's not look at sex as "who gives in to whom" or "who wins or loses" or which partner is "good or bad." It's important to consider the various approaches and the feelings and outcomes that may come packaged with each one. Again, in the *Sex Starved Marriage*, Michelle Weiner points out that the spouse with the lower desire for intimacy sets the pace. So these strategies are geared toward the spouse with lower desire to find more balance and satisfaction for both you and your spouse. All of them are underscored with the idea and philosophy of living deliberately.

Cultivating Sexual Willingness

Sex may be quick and not very romantic, or it may be filled with passion, foreplay, and a strong emotional connection. Sexual willingness is just that, a willingness to show up and have a sexual experience with your partner. If you and your partner are currently in a no-sex holding pattern, you should set a time for an intimate session—and then you both have to show up! You may find yourself feeling scared, anxious, or even a bit awkward. This is part of achieving intimacy in general, not just sexual intimacy. It is being willing to come to the table as your true self, without fleeing from or avoiding the situation.

You may alleviate some of this anxiety by simply sharing with your partner how nervous you are. Maybe you make it to the bed and just kiss, and that is your sexual interaction that day. Wherever you are in this process, cultivating a willingness starts with simply opening yourself to sexual experiences. The more experiences you have, the greater your willingness will become (similar to the gym—you may not always feel like going but you are willing to go) with more desire accompanying the willingness. Additionally, you may want to set a schedule of sorts to help create frequent-enough experiences that you start to make headway. Also, keep in mind that it is normal for women not to be aroused *prior* to being sexually intimate but become aroused as the sexual intimacy progresses.

REAL RELATIONSHIP TIP!
Learn to Speak a Second Language

Imagine you and your spouse speak two different languages, such as Spanish and English. Although you have a working knowledge of your spouse's language, it is still your second language and doesn't come as natural. We all have a primary "love language" as well that comes naturally for us but may be "foreign" to our spouse.

Dr. Chapman contributed greatly to the health of relationships by identifying what he calls "The Five Languages of Love." He identified five primary ways that everybody feels and receives love. We often love our spouses the way we want to be loved because that's what we understand. For example, if you receive love through physical touch, you are most likely physically affectionate with your spouse. If you feel love through receiving gifts, you may give little gifts, such as leaving little notes or finding something that reminded you of your spouse while you were out. However, just because you recognize love one way doesn't mean your spouse does. This is where selfless learning becomes important.

If you speak Spanish and your spouse speaks English, but neither deigns to learn the other's language, how successful will your marriage be? You literally wouldn't be able to communicate about bills, groceries, and any other necessary topic! There would be a lot of misunderstanding, loneliness, and difficulty knowing what the other wanted because you wouldn't understand each other. Knowing your primary love language and learning your spouse's love language immediately creates a sense of understanding and adds depth to your relationship. The following is a list of Dr. Chapman's love languages with a short description of each:

Words of Affirmation: If you enjoy receiving compliments, hearing your spouse say "I love you," or hearing expressions of gratitude, this may be how you primarily feel love.

Acts of Service: Doing something to ease the burden of life's everyday tasks and challenges will go a long way to the person who feels love through acts of service. This may be randomly washing the car, folding the laundry, or doing yard work.

Physical Touch: The person who finds himself or herself wanting to hug, hold hands, or share in sexual intimacy most likely experiences love through physical touch and affection.

Quality Time: Spending time together—whether playing a game, talking, or going for a walk—are all meaningful ways to show love to the person who values quality time.

Gifts: Regardless of the size or amount of gifts, it's the thought that counts. Receiving a gift sends the message to those who experience love this way, that your spouse was thinking about you!

While we can all probably relate to some of the languages on the list, there is usually one that feels more relevant to you and your spouse. Remember what you've learned in this chapter on living deliberately? Actively and deliberately learn your spouse's language and make "love" a verb. We highly recommend adding Dr. Chapman's book to your relationship library, using it to learn more about you and your spouse. It can be found at any major book store or online.

Life offers many transitions as we grow together in love and intimacy. What is intimacy in your teens and twenties is far from what becomes intimacy in the last four or five decades of life. Intimacy can become just being in the same room, holding hands at church, or a touch in the car as you drive, or a touch that reaches across to one another while saying good night. Occasional intercourse not ending in orgasm can be bonding and of great comfort to aging adults. Sexual playfulness is important, reminding each other that you are still chosen, attractive, and desired. Tenderness while accomplishing mutual tasks is beautiful and fulfilling. A tender compliment, an unexpected note, or a word of kindness at a difficult time can be a demonstration of emotional intimacy. Sexual contact usually diminishes with age; however, intimacy can grow and increase when sexual interaction is no longer the goal or the be all, end all.

Debra and James

Debra and James hadn't had sex in a long time. In fact, they realized it had been almost a year since they had been intimate. Both were so caught up with work, kids, church callings, and life that most nights they just fell into bed exhausted. The few times either of them made an attempt to initiate anything, the other came up with some excuse to avoid having sex. After a while, both of them just quit trying, jokingly resolving to "get back to it sometime." That "sometime" just never seemed to ever come.

Debra was perfectly fine with this situation, but James started to become anxious and resentful. While Debra could sense his frustration, she remarked to one of her friends that she just didn't "know how to pump up her desire enough to choose wanting sex with James over going to sleep."

Debra wanted things to change, but she wasn't sure how. The "willingness" on Debra's part led her to actively decide to drink a Coke during the evening so she would actually have more energy at bedtime. That night she was awake and energetic but still wasn't "turned on" like she thought she had to be in order to be intimate. However, Debra decided to wear something pretty to bed and just see what happened.

James definitely noticed the change and also decided to be hopeful things would progress. As he began kissing and caressing Debra, she began to feel stronger feelings of desire, which led her to want to go further. James noticed this and got more into it as well.

After having a great reunion, Debra joked that she owed it all to the Coke she drank that evening. James joked that he was going to buy her a case of Coke if it meant they could be intimate more than once a year! They felt more emotionally and physically connected than they had in a long time.

Acknowledging and Breaking the Auto Response

You and your partner may have such an established pattern of rejecting offers for sex because you haven't "felt like it" for so long, you reject it without thinking. Take a step back during your day and think about your reaction to sex. Is this something that is so well-practiced and personally ingrained that it has become a new norm? Here are some steps to take if this is the case:

1) Consider visualizing in your mind how you would like to respond if your spouse were to approach you for an intimate encounter.

2) Once you have that image, consider rehearsing this response in your mind so when your partner approaches you, you have already run through the scenario in which you accept his offer.

3) Consider sharing with your partner your willingness to start being open to his sexual invitations. This way he'll understand your intentions, and it will give both of you room to learn this new approach. Perhaps your auto response will still come, which triggers your partner's auto response. Yet when you both acknowledge it and have the patience and forgiveness to try again, it will be there for you.

How to Respond If You Have Been Rejected Numerous Times

Keep in mind, if you are the partner constantly being rejected, you too have an auto response. Part of your work is to identify your response and disrupt it in the same way. Maybe you are so used to being rejected, you immediately become angry or simply roll over and give the silent treatment. Maybe your partner rejects you but then acknowledges his auto response and would like to try again. Are you willing to start shifting your own auto responses or at least give them a closer look? There is a mutual responsibility to be willing and vulnerable in order to create a new action or reaction.

This vulnerable scenario occurs when you both lower your defenses. Change is a difficult thing. It requires risks and demands new thinking in both of you. You must gain the capacity to once again take the necessary steps. This process can hurt, but a little discomfort can be worth a new connection and to rekindle a relationship whose fire has grown dim.

Start Creating New Positive Experiences

Maybe you and your spouse have a long history of initiation and rejection, extended periods of abstinence, or painful sex, and so on. You may have many negative experiences within your sexual relationship. You may feel overwhelmed or resigned to the situation. Part of the healing process is making a choice and deliberately starting to create new, positive experiences.

Setting the stage may be an important aspect of having a positive outcome. What would that look like for both of you? Let's say you have an ongoing pattern of going to bed at 10:30 p.m., then one of you tries to initiate touching or spooning and the other rejects. You both roll over with a giant gap between you, feeling frustration, disappointment, and tension. Though you are on opposite sides of this pattern, you both feel frustrated that it continues to play out the same way night after night, week after long week. Decide to break your pattern. Maybe you schedule a date night, go to dinner, have satisfying conversation, and then plan on creating a new pattern of intimacy.

The more positive experiences you have, the more those start to create a new history and become the new norm in your relationship. Part of creating positive experiences will be considering the variables and putting the odds in your favor.

Consider the Variables—Put the Odds in Your Favor

Considering the variables doesn't mean looking for the ideal, because once you start having school, work, kids, sleep disruptions, and so on, the ideal doesn't exist. It simply means considering what you both have going on in your individual and collective lives and finding times and circumstances where you can come together sexually, in a way that is comfortable and doable.

You have to put the odds in your favor. For example, if you attempt to have sex at midnight after a long day, or if you are insensitive to your partner's stresses, the odds of having a successful encounter are not in your favor. It does not have the capacity or energy to produce anything else. Creating the five-minute sexual opportunities, in addition to your lengthier romantic scenarios, will allow for a more realistic take on sexuality, within the demands and complicated dynamics of modern life.

Make Connection a Priority

We have to make having a positive sexual relationship a priority because the demands of everyday living—career, child-bearing, family, church—will take as much time and energy as we permit. Examine where your sexual and emotional relationships are on your priority list—look at the physical and spiritual aspects as well. Is it something that you know you need to get to but rarely do because you have so many other things occupying your time and energy? If this is the case, consider moving it up on your priority list and schedule it as you would a meeting or lunch date. While this may seem like it takes out the romance, it puts the sexual connection back as an important part of your relationship to you and your spouse.

There is no better time than now to do this important work. If you keep putting it off, you may never get to it until the time for these things have past.

Increase Your Sexual IQ, Comfort, and Confidence

Look at an area in your life where you feel the most knowledgeable. For example, your career required obtaining a certain amount of education and training. There were books to read, classes to attend, and tests to take. All these experiences added to your ability to acquire the needed skills and perform your job. Sexual intimacy is similar. While our bodies are designed for sex, we may not have a clear understanding of what to do and how to do it. It's not shameful to read books, attend classes, or seek counseling for something so important. Another part of developing your intimacy IQ is asking your partner what she likes— she is going to be your *best* source of information.

You might be reading this book to increase your intimacy IQ. Knowledge is power. It allows you to develop a comfort and confidence. Most new things start out uncomfortable and become comfortable once we have time and continued exposure. Confidence comes as we take risks and apply some of our new knowledge.

Allow for the Learning Curve

Some learning curves are steeper than others. Whenever we are gaining knowledge, there may be growing pains. Creating space for the learning curve allows for mistakes and fumbles that will inevitably come. If you enter into your intimate relationship with the idea of learning, you will have the confidence to keep trying. Sexual intimacy is a pursuit that is never fully learned. It offers a lifetime worth of learning, letting go, losses, more learning, and growth.

Think about all the things you've have had to learn throughout your life. What if you never rode a bike again after crashing that first time? What if you hadn't continued learning to read just because you didn't feel like you were good at it? What if you quit those piano lessons after your first recital or stopped playing soccer after your first lost game? You already know how to learn something new. You try, fail, try again, maybe do okay, try again, fail, try again, get better, and so on. Learning how to be intimate is no different. It isn't easy, but it can be worth it. In the eternal perspective with our relationships, we are in the infancy of our learning.

Keep Your Sense of Humor

An important part of intimacy is keeping your sense of humor. Much of our bodily functions are not within our control. Stumbles are inevitable and can, if we let them, make for great memories. For example, have you ever tried a new recipe that failed miserably and you ended up ordering a pizza instead? Did you stop cooking? Did you blame yourself unnecessarily or say that you were just not cut out for making a meal for your family? We hope you were able to laugh and say, "Well, that didn't work out!" and you either tried that recipe again or decided, no matter how you cooked it, it wasn't going to be added to your recipe collection. Keeping your sense of humor can facilitate risk, vulnerability, positive experiences, and the learning curve.

Jamie and Ben

Jamie and Ben were so nervous to be intimate the first time that they decided to have all the lights off. They made things as dark as possible and could hardly see anything at all. What they thought would make for a less-embarrassing moment was quite the opposite. Jamie ended up tripping on a nearby chair on the way to the bed, causing her knee to bleed quite badly. On his way over to help her, Ben tripped over Jamie and landed, in a naked heap, on top of her. By the time they got the lights on, Jamie had bled all over Ben, herself, and the carpet! They spent the next few moments, completely naked, with the lights on, cleaning blood off the carpet so they wouldn't have to pay the hotel to have it repaired! Needless to say, they still laugh about that one. They both found, while embracing at the sink after cleaning off the blood, that intimacy was far more fun and less rigid than what they had supposed before the injured knee.

Living deliberately is about making a conscious choice to engage your spouse in intimacy—whether it's emotional, physical, spiritual, or sexual. It's moving love from simply being a feeling to a verb. It's choosing to prioritize your spouse and your relationship needs. We know and understand if it were easy than it wouldn't be a problem for so many people. However, by finding one strategy you relate to or could see yourself implementing, you start a healthy pattern of connection and create a spirit of love, safety, and intimacy.

THE NUTS AND BOLTS

A common phenomenon among people is to avoid the things they don't *feel* like doing. You can see this in everyday examples like going to the gym or confronting a coworker about a problem. As it relates to sexual intimacy, people who don't feel like having sex often wait until they *do* feel like it—which can lead to a prolonged period without it. This chapter introduces the idea or rule commonly known as "living deliberately." Living deliberately means that in relationships we learn to do certain things regardless of if you *feel* like doing them or not. This moves you past the stuck place of, "I just don't feel like it." These are the strategies discussed throughout the chapter to help cultivate a desire to be sexually intimate with your spouse:

Cultivate sexual willingness by scheduling opportunities to be intimate and be willing to step up and show up.

Acknowledge and break the auto response. You and your partner may have an established pattern in your intimacy of rejecting offers for sex because you haven't "felt like it" for so long, without even pausing to see if you are open for a sexual experience.

Start creating new positive experiences. If most of your negative sexual experiences have happened in the bedroom at precisely 10:30 p.m., it's time to try something different! A weekend away, morning sex, or whatever you can come up with.

Make connection a priority. We find time to do the things we want to do. Period. The "I'm too busy for this" excuse doesn't fly.

Increase your sexual IQ, comfort, and confidence. Knowledge is power. The more you know and understand about your body, your partner's body, and the process of intimacy—physically and emotionally—the more comfortable and confident you'll become.

Allow for the learning curve. Everything is a learning process—everything.

Keep your sense of humor. So, let's say things are getting hot-and-heavy and you trip and fall on the way to the bed. It doesn't have to ruin things if you can both keep your sense of humor.

Add sexual discussion to your conversation. You talk about work, kids, and church. Adding sex to your conversation is important.

Chapter Questions for Real-Life Application

1. What makes you feel loved? Write down all the ways you felt loved

growing up and now within your marriage. Think of concrete examples that you can share with your spouse.

2. How do you and your spouse differ on what feels like love to you both?

3. If intimacy is a verb, what are things you could do, starting today, that would bring you closer to your spouse?

4. If you feel stuck in one area of your relationship, look at the four aspects of the intimacy pyramid identifying comfortable areas while increasing your "deliberate" efforts in those less comfortable.

13

BABIES, BLENDING, AND INFERTILITY

*No matter how a child comes (or doesn't come)
into your life, it will affect your relationship*

C HILDREN BRING AN INCREDIBLE AMOUNT OF JOY AND HAPPI-
ness to a relationship. They also bring financial, emotional,
and mental strain as you work to provide for their needs in a
variety of areas. This can take a toll on your relationship, as you have
less time for each other. Anytime a child is brought into the home,
through whatever means, there will be a major adjustment. Learning
to navigate these waters will require creativity, patience, humor, and
the ability to recognize that your relationship still needs attention—
and lots of it.

Adoption/Foster Children

Let's start with adoptive or foster parents who may mistakenly
believe that children's impacts on their relationships are less then for
biological parents. In fact, there can be greater strain on your relationship due to the emotional roller coaster of adoption or the uncertainty
of foster care—not to mention the issues you already dealt with leading
to your decision to seek your children through a different avenue.

There is still the nervous anticipation of bringing someone new
into your home and heart. There will probably still be sleepless

nights, arguments over parenting decisions, new roles to consider, as well as whatever special emotional circumstances there may be with regards to adoption and foster care. Don't expect your relationship to smoothly sail through without any difficulty. Obviously there could be books (and there are) written on this subject. While the majority of this chapter is focused on pregnancy and the changes that brings, the suggestions at the end of the chapter will still be good for you to consider as you transition into parenthood. Also, please recognize that postpartum depression can occur among non-biological parents.

Infertility

According to the Center for Disease Control, since 2002, approximately 2.1 million women have been diagnosed as infertile or unable to conceive for twelve consecutive months. Infertility in a marriage can put a strain on elements of intimacy—adding additional anxiety to an already stressful situation. Spontaneity and pleasure can be replaced with calculation and "business." However, intimacy can be achieved and shared through the difficult trial of infertility.

Here are a few tips to consider (however, for more in-depth information on this subject, look at our resource section):

Nurture your relationship. If Noah would have neglected to maintain the ark in preparation for the animals coming on board causing it to sink, it wouldn't have done the animals any good. Finding ways to love, focus your attention on, and care for your spouse in non-sexual ways can help foster positive connections through a difficult time.

Find times to regularly talk and check-in with each other. Having a weekly conversation where you have a chance to share frustrations or difficulties, while also discussing the positive things working in your relationship, will help.

Be creative with other forms of intimacy. Sexual intimacy can turn from pleasure to procreation as you are working to becoming pregnant. However, by taking time to share longer hugs, passionate kisses, foot or hand massages, cuddling, and so on, you can continue to express your love and desire for closeness.

Pregnancy

Just as you are getting settled into your intimate life with each other, a new challenge presents itself! The little stick shows a plus sign indicating that the sex you've been enjoying has also been building something besides closeness. Pregnancy is one of the wonderful results of having sex and is a reason to celebrate a new life, but it will change your intimate relationship profoundly.

Rachelle and TJ

A few weeks after Rachelle found out she was pregnant, the morning sickness really hit. Rachelle said she felt like throwing up all day, every day, for several weeks and that even looking at food would sometimes make her feel queasy. She said that she could sometimes gain a reprieve from the nausea if she just sat still and didn't move. When her husband, TJ, would see her, he would want to hug and kiss her and just be around her. She tried to explain to him about just needing to sit still and hoped he wouldn't take it personally. She told him that she hoped to feel better in a few weeks and could then enjoy his great hugs again. TJ took it well and found other ways to help. They discovered that a snack of crackers and cheese would allow Rachelle to feel well enough that they could cuddle on the couch for awhile, watching TV, until the nausea hit again. TJ, in the meantime, learned some patience, which was going to be a trait he would need once he became a father.

The changes that occur during pregnancy affect the woman in an obvious way; they're more subtle in the man but can't be overlooked. Some women get so wrapped up in the changes they are experiencing, they forget their husband is also involved and may be feeling a little lost himself. Major hormone changes that affect a woman's desire to be intimate at all, and nausea, isn't an aphrodisiac. Some women are nauseated their entire pregnancy and unable to be intimate. After all, no one wants to throw up, or be thrown up on, during sex! The list of possible complications and changes during pregnancy is too long to list here. Let's discuss pregnancy in its three trimesters:

Zero to Twelve Weeks

Major internal changes are taking place. The placenta is growing, which requires a large amount of energy. Women generally feel unusually tired the first few weeks. Nausea, if it's going to occur, will begin sometime in this period. Combine nausea with fatigue and you don't necessarily have a recipe for a lot of great sex with your spouse. Of course intercourse is physically possible, barring complications, but the sexual buffet may be different, even unappetizing. These few weeks are fantastic for dreaming about your future child, cuddling, and enjoying other forms of intimacy with your spouse.

Twelve to Twenty-Four Weeks

If there is a honeymoon phase of pregnancy, this is it. Generally the nausea will decrease or stop, some energy will be regained, and the woman hasn't reached the bowling pin stage. This trimester can be a time of reconnection physically, if all is proceeding without complications. And, ladies, be aware that many men find their pregnant wives to be extremely attractive. They love the way your body is changing as your breasts and hips become more full. The "glow" you receive from all the pregnancy hormones make you look healthy and full of life—which you literally are. This can be a time to show off your new body and enjoy a new experience in your lovemaking.

Twenty-Four to Forty Weeks

By about week thirty, the growing fetus begins to really be on display. And by week thirty-five, most women are starting to feel really uncomfortable. Sex at this point definitely has its pros and cons. If the pregnancy is progressing without complications, most couples can safely have sex for as long as they both feel comfortable. In fact, semen is full of prostaglandins, or chemicals, which can actually help get labor going. However, as the pregnancy nears its end, the pelvis, hips, legs, and just about every other point on a woman's body can become extremely uncomfortable, making sex uncomfortable as well. The bulging belly can make it nearly impossible to have sex in the traditional missionary style.

In addition, the vulva, labia, and clitoris begin to be more engorged with blood, which can make them either more or less sensitive to the touch. Good sexual positions at this point would be either with the woman lying on her side, with the man in "spooning" position behind her or with her on top, so she can better control the pace and depth of the thrust. Lastly, as the fetus drops lower into the pelvic region, the cervix may lower as well. This can be painful if the head of the penis is bumping up against the cervix. Intimacy during this time requires lots of communication, patience, and understanding.

Just know that once you embark on the wonderful and complex journey of pregnancy, you need to be mentally and emotionally prepared to accept the changes as they come. More than likely, the changes will be temporary. Let us repeat that. More than likely, the changes will be temporary! Those nine months may feel like forever, but they will come to an end. Looking for ways to connect during this time will help you through and prepare you for the years of "wonderful interruptions" a child will bring you. There are many books and articles that go into greater depth about the phases of pregnancy, hormone changes, and physical changes. See our resource section for ideas.

Postpartum Intimacy

Yay! The baby is here! If the labor and delivery went well, you were able to have a wonderful bonding moment with your spouse and new baby. Is there anything more intimate than watching someone you love bring life into this world? Or listening to the soothing voice of your husband and feeling the strength of his body as he helps you deliver your child? For some couples, the birthing process forever strengthens and enhances their intimacy. It presents her body in a new light. She may gain new awareness and feel even more comfortable with herself. He may see her using her body to produce his child and love her and her body even more.

On the other hand, a possible barrier to a return of normal intimacy after a baby is if the woman experiences postpartum depression or other emotional difficulties. Again, please take note that hormones are flying all over the place during conception, birth, and delivery. Add to that chronic sleep deprivation and transitioning to caring for a new person and you have a recipe for some serious issues that might need to be addressed.

In our well-meaning LDS culture, we sometimes place high expectations on our new mothers. Our pioneer heritage of just "pull yourself up by your bootstraps" can lead a woman to try to do and be too much too quickly after a baby is born—like returning to a demanding church assignment. This should be a time when we treat our new mothers gently and with care instead of pushing them to be up and going again too soon.

Sometimes serious problems can present themselves that require intervention and should not be ignored. The best way for a husband and wife to regain their relationship after a baby is born is to move slowly, gently, patiently, and with great understanding, remembering that "this too shall pass" and you will have more than enough time to enjoy each other once again.

REAL RELATIONSHIP TIP!
Postpartum Depression

According to Katherine Stone, founder of the website Postpartum Progress, postpartum depression takes a major toll on intimacy.

For most couples, intimacy and the frequency of intercourse changes for weeks or months after having a baby. After delivery, there is common discomfort and/or pain with intercourse for women, and most couples are exhausted after sleepless days and nights of caring for a newborn. Combine that with the demand of breastfeeding for those who go this route, and many couples will spend much less time being intimate. In fact, one study showed that 50 percent of women and 20 percent of men report reduced sexual responsiveness for 6–12 months postpartum. And one-third of couples will report this two to three years after birth. Women who are struggling with depression will have an extra challenge here as lowered libido is one of the very common symptoms of depression and at times a side-effect of antidepressant medication.

Since postpartum depression and anxiety will affect up to 30 percent of women and approximately 10 percent of men, we felt it was relevant to list the symptoms.

For women, if you are experiencing pregnancy-related depression or postpartum depression or anxiety, you might feel more angry or irritable, guilt, or extreme worries and fears often over the health and safety of the baby. You might experience panic attacks, a feeling of losing control, a lack of interest in your baby, changes in your eating and sleeping habits—not able to sleep when the baby sleeps, trouble concentrating, thoughts of hopelessness, or possibly thoughts of harming the baby or yourself.

For men, if you are experiencing postpartum depression, you might feel increased anger with others; have changes in weight; have loss of interest in things such as work, hobbies, or sex; experience frequent headaches, digestion problems, or pain, have problems with motivation or concentration; feel discouraged or easily stressed; feel a need for increased risk-taking; have increased concerns about productivity at home or work; or experience conflict over how you feel you should be as a man versus how you actually are.

For more information on pregnancy and postpartum depression and anxiety, see our resources section in the back of this book.

Bart and Michelle

Bart remembers watching Michelle deliver their first child, and the experience left him feeling pretty traumatized and unsure of how to even approach his wife's body. Things didn't go quite as planned and Michelle ended up with a C-section. Bart said he was unprepared for the way events went, as well as the various ways caregivers were examining Michelle's body, and then watching the C-section itself. He said it took him months to be able to feel anything sexual toward Michelle.

During the delivery, her body had seemed anything but sexual to him and just purely functional. However, after watching her heal from the birth and regain her strength, he found he enjoyed running his finger along her C-section scar because it became a symbol of what she was willing to sacrifice in order to deliver their child. Bart had just needed some time to adjust. Michelle, on the other hand, was perfectly okay with his lack of sexual desire because she was just too tired and sore to even think about being intimate for several months.

Let's talk about the first few weeks after a baby is born. Obviously everyone is tired and out of sorts. If the woman is breastfeeding, her breasts will become quite engorged, and her nipples may be quite painful while they are adjusting to the strong suck of the baby. While her uterus is healing, she will still bleed for several weeks postpartum and should be encouraged to refrain from vigorous sexual activity, if any at all. If she has had stitches due to a tear in the perineum (the skin linking the vagina and the anus) or other areas, she will be sore and will definitely need to abstain from any sex until given the go-ahead by her care provider. Generally a good time frame for trying to return to intimacy is about six weeks postpartum. Again, that is generally speaking—it could be longer.

A C-section recovery, a major episiotomy, or extensive "tear" would require a longer recovery time. You must take into account the labor and delivery, how you both are handling transitioning to a new baby, and the amount of sleep or lack thereof you both are experiencing. All these factors will contribute to your ability to be intimate.

Mike and Trisha

Although things had gone well for Trisha throughout her pregnancy, labor, and delivery, she had yet to regain her sense of self emotionally. She felt tired, flabby, and overwhelmed with all the changes involved with caring for two children. Additionally, she was also so "in love" with her new daughter and two-year-old son that she really didn't want to spend a lot of time with anybody else, including her husband. After several months, Mike began to notice he had been relegated to the bottom rung of Trisha's "ladder" and wasn't happy. He loved their new baby as well, but he wanted to be able to reconnect with Trisha and regain their sense of intimacy. When Mike approached Trisha, she promised to try but just didn't seem to have the desire or willingness and was tired from waking up to nurse their baby in the night.

When a woman is breastfeeding, the hormones that allow her body to create milk can also cause her to have a lower sexual desire. These hormones affect her emotionally and physically. Her vagina will be drier and may need some lubrication for her to have sex comfortably. If we think about this from an evolutionary perspective, this would make sense. Nature would want the woman to be able to feed that baby without having to worry about another pregnancy too soon.

Body Image

Pregnancy alters a woman's body forever. Never again will she have the same perky breasts, slim hips, or tight skin. Of course, some things can be regained through diet and exercise. However, imagine a balloon after it has been blown up. After the first time, the balloon can almost return to its original shape, but after the second, third, fourth, or eighth time, the balloon is irrevocably stretched into a new shape. Men, please be considerate and appreciative of your wife's "new" body. The last thing your wife will want is to have you grab her newly stretched out skin and move it around like you're kneading dough! This is a vulnerable time for her, and she will need your reassurance—especially during intimate moments.

Rich and Karen

Karen found herself trying to suck her stomach in every time Rich put his arms around her after the birth of their baby. She hated how her stomach felt doughy and stretchy. She wouldn't allow him to wrap his arms around her in bed because she was so afraid of what he would think. One of the things he had loved about her was her athletic body, and this stomach of hers was anything but! One time, after he noticed her pulling her stomach in, her asked her why she did that. After explaining, he lovingly placed his hands on her stomach and told her he loved her, all of her, and not just her stomach. He also expressed his appreciation for her willingness to sacrifice her body in order to create their beautiful child.

Our society demands too much of women when it comes to body image. Our bodies are gifts from God. We have the opportunity to bring life into this world, but we are required to make a sacrifice in order to receive the miracle. Our vanity, which can sometimes be a hindrance, is most definitely affected as a result of a pregnancy. Try to ignore a myriad of media images presented of women who have been airbrushed into perfection. They are not real; you are. And believe it or not, your husband wants a real flesh-and-blood woman, imperfections and all. So please, ease up on yourself, and you will find your intimate life can be even richer and fuller than before your baby was born.

After Kid 2, 3, 4, 5, 6, and So On

Some people joke that the more kids you have, the less sex you have, except for the fact that you keep having kids, so you must be having sex somehow. Couples with many children come to accept a few things about themselves and their sex lives:

1) Quicker can be better. Sometimes finding five minutes in the bathroom alone together can be all you need. Yes, the kids might be banging on the door wondering why you've locked yourselves in there, but you'll both come out smiling, which will make for happier parents the rest of the day! Don't be afraid to take advantage of little moments because you don't know when you might get them next. Besides, you'll feel like you've just "gotten away" with something and can give each other little knowing looks the rest of the day, which can be pretty fun.

2) Through thick and thin really means through thick and thin! With the birth of each child, Denise would joke with her husband that he was having the opportunity to be intimate with many women during their marriage because her body would be slightly different with each child! On a more serious note, Denise appreciated that her husband, Dan, was attracted to her despite the stretched-out skin on her stomach, stretch marks across her abdomen, saggy breasts due to breastfeeding, and wider hips and legs. Dan told her he saw her body as even more beautiful because of the children she had borne, as well as the way pregnancy and motherhood enhanced her beauty and made it more real. Besides, Dan had put on a few pounds himself and would joke that she was having to enjoy "more" of him and he hadn't even had a child himself!

3) Having sex once in a three-month period is okay. Really. Having kids, especially more than one, is a lot of work. There is a reason studies show marital satisfaction rises when each child leaves home. It's not that you don't love them; it's that you actually get to spend time with each other again and generally have a little more money to spend on each other.

When you have kids pulling on you all day, it can be tough to have anything left—emotionally, physically, and financially—for each other. Often, especially when your children are young, you are either falling into bed exhausted, or you have at least one child in bed with you! A month or two can pass without you even knowing it. Again, don't worry; with some effort, you will find your way back to each other (foot rubs also really help).

4) There are more options than just sexual intercourse. So often we get hung-up on that "six week" appointment because that is when our wives are *finally* given the go ahead to have sex. However, there is no need to wait six weeks to be intimate. You can kiss, cuddle, hug, and attempt to try other forms of intimacy. Again, if sex is like dining, try another section of the buffet.

5) Up the intimacy in other areas. Remember in the living deliberately chapter where we talk about the different chemicals that help attachment and desire? Studies show that a longer hug can actually produce oxytocin or those "cuddle hormones" we all love so much.

6) Allow yourself to feel awkward or uncomfortable but don't let that stand in your way. Again, it's not abnormal to get out of a sexual "groove" in the weeks before and after the baby is born. It's a matter of finding and creating a new groove. This is where living deliberately can really help because most often it's not going to be "desire" kicking off the sexual intimacy. However, with a little willingness and patience, you can cultivate that desire to be close to your spouse and rekindle your connection and relationship with each other.

No matter how they come, children are wonderful additions to your family. Even though your relationship will change, it will usually change for the better. You can come to love and appreciate each other more deeply than you thought possible.

THE NUTS AND BOLTS

One of the possible wonderful consequences of your marital relationship is adding a new member to your family—either through pregnancy, adoption, or step-children. No matter how they get there, children change all the rules of the game. If, however, your struggle is with infertility, the sorrow and pain of that journey can greatly impact your relationship as well.

A pregnant woman is a whole new experience. The list of physical and hormonal changes that take place, as well as possible complications, is too long to list. Be prepared to experience a new kind of intimacy with your spouse. For example, some women spend the entire nine months throwing up! Vomit is definitely not conducive to intimacy. However, you can find ways to support her physically and emotionally, which will still enhance your relationship. Just remember, pregnancy doesn't last forever. Enjoy it while you can.

Postpartum intimacy (after the baby has arrived) presents its own unique opportunities. With both of you feeling tired, overworked, impatient, and unsure of all the changes happening, this is a good time to take things slowly, gently, and with great patience. Women are especially insecure about their bodies at this time and need their spouses to be extra supportive as they adjust to their new, more womanly body. Ladies, don't forget your spouses are adjusting too. He needs to be treated with the same patience and kindness you want. And don't forget he still needs the same amount of love and affection he did before the baby was born—just like you.

Step, adopted, and foster children also bring dramatic changes and adjustment. In fact, there can be greater strains on your relationship due to the emotional roller coaster of adoption or the uncertainty of foster care, not to mention the issues you already dealt with leading to your decision to seek your children through a different avenue.

Infertility can place a strain on elements of intimacy within the marriage, adding additional anxiety to an already stressful situation. Spontaneity and pleasure can be replaced with calculation and "business" and something private and intimate becomes sterile and public. However, intimacy can be shared and maintained.

Chapter Questions for Real-Life Application

1. How has having/not having children impacted your intimacy? Are you okay with the adjustments made, or are there some unresolved areas?

2. What do you do to keep your relationship the highest priority in the home? What steps could be taken to show your spouse he or she is #1 on your list? A hug? A date? A phone call? Pick something and do it.

3. When was the last time your told your spouse you loved him, or thought her beautiful, in front of your children (testimony meeting doesn't count)? If it has been a while, demonstrate how you feel about each other in front of your children. It's good for them to see it.

14

GUILT, SHAME, AND SECRECY

Feeling bad for feeling good and the "good girl/bad boy" syndrome

Guilt, Shame, and Secrecy

NYONE WHO IS HAVING A HUMAN EXPERIENCE UNDERSTANDS what it is to feel guilt. While it may not be a pleasant feeling, it is healthy and helps us ultimately be our best selves. Guilt is a natural part of the human experience. Guilt reminds us when we have gone against our morals and values. It's what drives us to engage the world in a kind, humane, and honest way. It fosters humility and provides empathy. It keeps our self-esteem intact and allows us to accept ourselves—including all our flaws. We can allow for God to love us as we are, as whole beings with strengths and flaws.

Now on the flip side, anyone having a human experience will also more than likely understand what it's like to feel shame, or to feel like our self-worth has been diminished due to our actions or behaviors. Shame subtly intertwines what we do with who we are. It can cause us to feel that if we are less-than-perfect, that we are inadequate. We divide ourselves into "good" and "bad" and don't see ourselves as whole, imperfect beings, reliant on the Atonement to make it through this life. It turns us from feeling God's love and changes self-love to self-hate. It makes us feel undeserving. It can cause us to turn away from relationships and opportunities for intimacy and can breed depression. Many members of the LDS faith experience guilt to such a degree that it moves from healthy to debilitating, and it causes embedded feelings of low self-esteem and self-worth. It fosters the feeling that we are not worthy of others' love, let alone God's love. This experience is especially true when it comes to our sexuality. Satan has done a wonderful job of creating so much confusion, misunderstanding, and perversion surrounding sex, it can be hard to discern and healthily navigate these waters.

In his book *Doctrinal Insights to the Book of Mormon*, Douglas Bassett notes, regarding the foundation of our faith that, "Jesus Christ always builds us up and never tears us down." Christ is the author of our imperfection, being a sign of our humanity and not an illustration of our worth. President Monson shared, "When we remember that each of us is literally a spirit son or daughter of God, we will not find it difficult to approach our Heavenly Father in prayer. He appreciates the value of this raw material which we call life. 'Remember the worth of souls is great in the sight of God' (D&C 18:10)." His pronouncement inspires purpose in our lives.

Furthermore, Elaine S. Dalton of the general Relief Society presidency said,

> You may not have heard the Lord call you by name, but He knows each one of you and He knows your name. Elder Neal A. Maxwell said, "I testify to you that God has known you individually . . . for a long, long time (see D&C 93:23). He has loved you for a long, long time. He not only knows the names of all the stars (see Psalm 147:4; Isaiah 40:26); He knows your names and all your heartaches and your joys!"
>
> Since Adam and Eve, Heavenly Father has given us continual messages that he loves and cares for us. Not just our good parts, but all parts of us. Can you think of any greater love than willingly sending your son to be crucified in order to bring forth the salvation of all your children? Our mortal life is a journey filled with missteps and faults. We have the opportunity to view our mistakes as a way to learn and grow.

Zach and Emma

A couple of years into their marriage, Zach and Emma got into what they called their "doozy" of a fight. They were both tired, over-worked, and Zach was feeling last on Emma's list as she spent most of the time trying to care for their two children. One night, after a long day at work, Zach's coworkers talked him into hitting the local bar with them to unwind. Zach had previously declined all invitations, but this night, he decided he had had enough and deserved a break. He went with the guys to what he thought was just a bar but was actually a strip bar. Zach had never been to one before and immediately felt out of place and embarrassed. At the same time, he was overwhelmed with the sights and sounds of the place and stayed longer than he realized. By the time he got home, he felt horrible and had resolved not to tell Emma.

Soon, however, with the frustrations at home and at work continuing, Zach started to think back on his experience at the bar and felt like he wanted to go back. This thought was immediately coupled with an image of Emma, at home with their children, that brought him more feelings of guilt and shame. Zach decided he wouldn't go back but struggled with still feeling locked out of Emma's life. He decided he must be a terrible husband and father if he would even consider going back to the bar. The cycle of guilt and shame had set in for Zach, causing him to pull further away from Emma, which caused her to get even more involved with the kids. By the time they sought counseling, they were pretty entrenched in their cycle and needed help to get out.

Unfortunately, one of the side effects of toxic shame, or the shame that attacks our self-worth, is secrecy and fear. Secrecy is not gender specific and is one of Satan's best tools to isolate ourselves from others. This type of secrecy can make us feel dirty, weird, or as if we are the *only* one feeling the way we feel, or making the mistakes we are. If we are feeling we are "bad" for something we have done, our initial response will not be to share this with anybody and to hold it inside. We hide ourselves from others and hide our behaviors. Fear of the unknown or the response can keep us from approaching our spouse or reaching out for help.

We may have a dual-self in which we are engaging in behaviors that our spouse doesn't know about. This is not the same idea as privacy or boundaries. These are behaviors that we feel we would be "caught" or "embarrassed" or "ashamed" if anyone found out. These behaviors are an attempt to try to numb our feelings to avoid feeling the shame, through substance abuse, rage or contempt, addictive behaviors, compulsive shopping or eating, or whatever the case may be. It's the way we are trying to get away from our worthlessness in a secretive manner so no one knows just how "awful" we are. This is where the beginning of the shame cycle starts. It's when, as Jennifer Hoffman so eloquently puts it, "We deny our divinity."

"Good Girl Syndrome"

Another aspect of shame and guilt is the "good girl syndrome." We could write an entire book on this topic alone because the good girl syndrome stretches beyond just sexuality. But for the sake of this book, we will be focusing on the sexual aspect. Laura Brotherson states the following in her book *And They Were Not Ashamed*:

> The "Good Girl Syndrome" is a result of the negative conditioning that occurs from parents, church, and society as they teach—or fail to teach—the goodness of sexuality and its divine purposes. This conditioning leads to negative thoughts and feelings about sex and the body, resulting in an inhibited sexual response within marriage . . . The Good Girl Syndrome may be the great underlying and underestimated because of sexual dissatisfaction in marriage. (Brotherson 2)

Due to cultural, religious, and family influences, we all come to a marriage with a sexual history—whether we've had sex or not.

Remember our chapter on identifying your sexual history? Part of your sexual history may not have been direct at all, but indirect messages you picked up and internalized in church, school, or in your home. Women are taught to be the "gatekeepers" of boys sexuality. That it's up to them to keep boys in check, hold the boundaries, and dress in a way that doesn't plant sexual thoughts.

Scripturally speaking, there isn't a strong example of healthy female sexuality. Women are typically depicted as pure and virgins, or prostitutes and seductresses. Those two messages are confusing because we are taught and commanded to cleave to our spouses. Remember the Young Women's lesson where you were asked if you wanted a piece of chewed-up gum? The moral of the lesson was to stay morally clean so you weren't like a piece of chewed-up gum, giving a negative image of sexual activity. While this lesson may have been well-meaning, how do you resolve in marriage being taught the idea of being a piece of chewed-gum even though now sexual activity is technically "okay"?

REAL RELATIONSHIP TIP!
Examine Your "Shoulds"

Ever notice the "shoulds" in your life? The "shoulds" comprise the internal list we keep of all of the things we "should" be doing but are not—or not to the standard we "should" be. Our shoulds create anxiety, guilt, and can contribute to low self-esteem. We may not even be aware of the shoulds that are ruling our life. They seem to hang around like a bad odor you can't find the source of!

If, on the other hand, we are aware of them, we probably haven't examined them thoroughly to decide their importance. Our shoulds come from church, family, and society. For example, we "should" read our scriptures, pray daily, and attend church regularly. Shoulds can be healthy and motivating if transformed to "I would like to" or "I choose to." Maggie, recently married, went to Easter dinner at her mother's house. Just like every other Easter dinner, her grandparents, aunts, uncles, and cousins were there. However, this year it was Maggie's turn to prepare the Easter ham. She was nervous to prepare such an important dish but felt prepared because she had been taught by her mom while growing up.

Maggie pulled out a large pan and proceeded to cut a large chunk off the end of the ham to discard. Her grandma gasped and asked her why she was wasting all of that good meat? Maggie looked at her mom and said, "Because that's how my mom prepared it." Maggie's mom looked at *her* mom and said, "I cut it off because that's how *you* prepared it." Maggie's grandma, with a soft smile and a light laugh said, "I only cut off the end of the ham because I never had a pan big enough to cook it."

The shoulds in our life are a lot like this story. We live by certain rules because we always have—they are all we have known. However, if we don't stop and look at them, understand where they come from, and whether they work for us, we may be cutting off "good ham" unnecessarily simply because "we should."

Make a list of the different shoulds in your life, including your sexual shoulds. Keep the beneficial ones and throw the rest out!

Amy and Tom

One night, not long after they were married, Amy and Tom were enjoying an intimate romp on the couch. This was a first for them. Up to that point, their usual spot was in the bedroom, with the lights off, in the traditional missionary position. Amy got caught up in the moment and allowed herself to be "carried away" with her feelings. Afterward, Amy hurriedly grabbed her clothes, covered herself, and quickly ran to the bathroom and locked the door. She couldn't believe she had just "had sex" on the couch without any thought or hesitation! She felt horrible and that she had just done something wrong. After all, nothing about what just happened was in any way "pure" or "spiritual" as she had been taught. It was "telestial."

When she tried to explain her feelings to Tom, he couldn't understand where she was coming from and felt like nothing was wrong with what had just occurred. After talking to a few people, Amy realized a *lot* of people have sex on the couch—as well as other areas—and they were still good people! She began to work through some of her perceptions in order to blend what she had been taught concerning sexual intimacy with the reality of now being a married adult with stewardship over her own sexuality.

Furthering the mixed messages, most of us were taught that sex, or any sexuality, was bad until marriage. When we reached our wedding night we had to make a paradigm shift in our thinking. We went from refraining from "inappropriate contact" with our fiancé just the night before, to touch not only being appropriate, but fun, healthy, and acceptable. It's safe to assume it's going to be difficult for a woman to resolve feeling bad for feeling good, or not even feeling good about having had anything to do with sex.

By cleaving unto our spouses, then aren't we leaving the idea of being pure and virtuous? This can leave us to feeling bad and dirty, especially when we do find ourselves enjoying it. "Good girls" shouldn't actually want sex or desire sex but want to have sex to have babies and to please their husbands. It can place women on a narrow and difficult path by being sexy but not *too* sexy, by being sexual but not *too* sexual, by being available but not *too* available. As one woman so articulately put it, "My head is not okay with what my body is doing."

Unless you came from a home where you were openly and actively taught about healthy sexuality, or fortunate enough to have Young Women's and general church leaders who were able to teach this, most women carry this experience around on some level. While we all want to be our best possible selves, it's important to include being sexual beings as part of an idea of "the good girl." So, what do you do to find a space where you can accept all of the possibilities?

"Bad Boy Syndrome"

Most of what was written above applies to the men as well. Men were also given certain messages pertaining to sex and sexuality that may be causing internal conflict or difficulty in marriage.

Cory

Cory was about three months into his marriage when he and his wife found out they were pregnant with their first child. While they both were planning and excited about the prospect of building their family, Cory was not ready for the changes in their sexual life that started to present themselves. Their sexual relationship was already strained, and his wife was struggling with feeling guilty about having sex. Over the course of the year, Cory's sexual frustration increased and he started playing with the idea of masturbating to relieve some of the tension. After much thought, and going back and forth between what in his mind was justification and guilt, he decided to try masturbating. He got to the point where he was about to climax, but stopped because he started to feel incredibly guilty. After this incident, despite his attempts to resolve this for himself, he started wondering if he needed to meet with his bishop to confess what he had done. Furthermore, he hadn't told his wife and felt guilty about this.

So, How Do You Work with This?

How do you overcome the "bad boy/good girl syndrome?" First, perform a self-assessment to understand any negative or shameful feelings about sexual intimacy. If you haven't already gone through the self-assessment exercise in the "Understanding Your Sexual History" chapter, now would be a good time to answer those questions and gain some personal insight. If you have held dirty or negative core beliefs about sexuality for most of your life, changing your perspective or adjusting your beliefs will take time and may include tearful moments after you have a sexual experience with your spouse.

If you understand this going in, you can find purpose in your efforts to be intimate with your spouse, knowing you are working through your feelings of shame or guilt. Allowing your spouse into this process, and not trying to hide your tears or pain, will also be an intimate and vulnerable experience that can bring you closer together. Husbands, don't take your wife's emotional response to sex as a personal rejection, but as something that needs to be healed in her. It is ultimately a "couple" issue, not just a "she" issue. Consider what messages you received as men regarding women's sexuality. Wives, consider what messages you received regarding men's sexuality. Trying to change perspective or core beliefs requires mental practice, personal empathy, and willingness to continue addressing them as they arise and a place of safety for vulnerability and our real selves to come forward.

Consider approaching your sexual interactions from a neutral position rather than going in with a negative approach such as "this is yucky," or "I don't like this." Give yourself room to experience instead of just having your body shut down before you even begin. Approach it from a place of neutrality.

Returning to the "how sex is like dining" analogy, there is nothing wrong with chocolate cake. It's delicious; however, if you were always taught that chocolate cake was bad, you would probably end up feeling guilty for not only eating it, but enjoying it as well. You would have to eat quite a few slices of that cake before you started to feel comfortable and relaxed and able to enjoy it. If your spouse were struggling with eating cake, would you berate her and take it personally? You would probably continue eating your chocolate cake and hope she would join in thoroughly enjoying it as well.

Find some affirmations pertaining to your sexuality that you can say to yourself daily. Additionally, challenge your negative thoughts and feelings when they present themselves. It will feel like it takes a lot of effort, but the pay-off will be worth it. Think of it as if you have spent a lot of your life exercising certain mental muscles and now you are trying to build up new ones. This book includes many ideas surrounding sexuality that you can jot down to create your own list of affirmations. Here are some to get you started:

I have inherent value as a child of God.

I am comfortable with my sexuality.

I am happy to be intimate with my spouse.

I enjoy my body and all the feelings associated with it.

I am going to relax and have fun being intimate with my spouse.

Remember, nothing is wrong with you for feeling this way; don't feel bad for feeling good. You are a woman or man of self-worth. We all have areas in our life that need adjustment and healing. For additional readings and resources on this topic, visit our resource section.

A note we will include for those who have married in or out of the temple with issues of not having kept the law of chastity as they understood it: Feelings of guilt, shame, secrecy, and so on stand to destroy the marriage. These circumstances are covered completely by the Atonement. Please be willing to forgive yourselves and your spouse. Don't allow mistakes of passion and love (so easy to fall into) to destroy what you both so desperately desire and deserve. Heavenly Father is not a God of hopelessness. Please get help to overcome these negative feelings if you are in such a situation. It is not worth going through a life together with this kind of pain. It is not what the Lord wants for either of you.

If you are in an abusive, coercive relationship or do not have a sense of safety, opening yourself up in this capacity can further put you in a

position of harm. If you are in this situation, consider seeking ecclesiastical or mental health support.

THE NUTS AND BOLTS

Anyone who is having a human experience understands what it
is to feel guilt. While guilt may not be a pleasant feeling, it is healthy
and helps us ultimately be our best selves. Guilt is a natural part of the
human experience. Guilt reminds us when we have gone against our
morals and values. It's what drives us to engage the world in a kind,
humane, and honest way. It keeps our self-esteem intact and allows us
to accept ourselves—including all our flaws. We can allow for God to
love us as we are, as whole beings, with strengths and flaws.

On the flip side, anyone having a human experience will also more
than likely understand what it's like to feel shame, or to feel like our
self-worth has been diminished due to our actions or behaviors. Shame
subtly intertwines what we do with who we are. It can cause us to feel
that if we are less-than-perfect we are inadequate. We divide ourselves
into "good" and "bad" and don't see ourselves as whole, imperfect
beings, reliant on the Atonement to make it through this life. It turns
us from feeling God's love and changes self-love to self-hate. It makes
us feel undeserving. It can cause us to turn away from relationships
and opportunities for intimacy, and can breed depression.

Unfortunately, one of the side effects of toxic shame, or the shame
that attacks our self-worth, is secrecy. Secrecy is not gender specific and
is one of Satan's best tools to isolate ourselves from others. This type
of secrecy can make us feel dirty, isolated, or as if we are the *only* one
feeling the way we feel, or making the mistakes we are. If we are feeling
we are "bad" for something we have done, our initial response will not
be to share this with anybody and to hold it inside. We hide ourselves
from others and hide our behaviors.

How do you overcome the "bad boy/good girl syndrome"? First,
perform a self-assessment to understand any negative or shameful feelings about sexual intimacy. If you haven't already gone through the
self-assessment exercise in the "Understanding Your Sexual History"
chapter, now would be a good time to answer those questions and gain

some personal insight. If you have held "dirty" or negative core beliefs about sexuality for most of your life, changing your perspective or adjusting your beliefs will take time and may include tearful moments after you have a sexual experience with your spouse.

Chapter Questions for Real-Life Application

1. Have you ever thought about the messages you were taught, or perceived, while growing up? Have they affected your ability to enjoy intimacy?

2. If you struggle with feelings of guilt, assess whether they are coming from the correct source. God-given guilt will motivate and inspire you to do better, while man-given or Satan-given guilt will make you feel hopeless and despairing.

3. Have you used guilt or shame in your relationship in order to control a situation?

15
PORNOGRAPHY

Understanding how pornography impacts your life and your intimacy

PORNOGRAPHY IS THE GREATEST MENTAL HEALTH AND SOCIAL problem in the religious life and community of our generation. That may seem like an exaggeration, but unfortunately it's not. Attention must be paid to this subject. If you think that just because you don't have an addiction to pornography and that it's not affecting you or your relationship, you are wrong. Pornography is everywhere. There's hardly a person who hasn't viewed, intentionally or not, some sort of pornography on TV, at the movies, or on the Internet. And, those images are instantly recalled—forever. There is a reason for this, which this chapter will cover. This is the reality of pornography, and you must pay attention.

Pornography is the greatest counterfeit in the world. Conspiring men and women, and the powers of evil and deception, have created pornography to distract us and move us away from relationships, marriage, and real intimacy. This incessant counterfeit destroys marriages and leaves its victims alone, frustrated, and trapped in a web from which many find it almost impossible to escape.

Pornography is a $12 billion industry in the United States. Over 3.5 billion dollars are spent annually for research and development in order to entice and entrap in its powerful grip people at every cultural, financial, and maturity level.

Pornography's greatest lie is that it provides guaranteed gratification every time we open it, look at it, read it, or allow a past visualization or sexual scenario to cross our minds. There is almost nothing in existence that can make that same claim. It does not require our full attention, our money, a clean shave, or even a brushed and bathed person. We can receive instant gratification even if we have not showered in two weeks. It doesn't and will not talk back. It demands nothing of us. It never requires a relationship. We don't have to talk to it or show any intelligence to obtain it or use it; we don't even have to leave our homes to download it, abuse it, and receive gratification from it at any time of the day or night.

In their book *Confronting Pornography*, Daniel Gray and Rory Reid provide a wonderful illustration of why Satan would use pornography to destroy the family.

> Consider our bodies. Satan will never have one. No wonder he would want us to devalue our bodies, to disrespect them. Consider the sacred nature of sex in marriage. Consider the bonding that takes place between a husband and a wife, and consider the wonderful opportunity to be able to bring children into this world and have a family. No wonder Satan would want us to degrade that. Pornography can distort the picture of who we really are and what we are really here for.

We talked about how Hollywood distorts our idea of what romance, relationships, and sexual intimacy are supposed to be like. Pornography makes these distortions seem like a PG movie. It objectifies people, making them inanimate objects without needs, quirks, and feeling. If people become objects, then they are there to satisfy and meet needs without challenge, opinion, or feeling. Furthermore, it takes gender and distorts the reality of what it is versus how the individual could be, not only sexually but out in the world. It creates the dangerous illusion that sex is the single most important aspect of a relationship, and not just sex, but sex in the way that they sell it. And last, it creates a habit of immediate gratification rather than time, effort, work, and communication—all the components that make up a meaningful, intimate relationship. It is the antithesis of relationship.

Todd and Angie

Todd and Angie hadn't been married long when Angie knew something was wrong. Their honeymoon had been awful, but Angie attributed it to lack of knowledge and experience and hoped things would get better. Todd had openly criticized her body and had difficulty maintaining an erection unless Angie was in a "specific position" each time they were intimate. Soon after their honeymoon, Angie noticed Todd spent a lot of time each evening on the computer and came to bed somewhat agitated and anxious. When they did try to have sex, Todd wanted Angie to try things she wasn't comfortable with yet and became angry when she wouldn't comply. He brought home specific clothing he wanted her to wear and eventually suggested they "check out some porn together" in order to bring their relationship "closer" as well as "teaching [Angie] a few things about sex."

Angie didn't think this seemed right but didn't know what to do. She still wasn't sure if this was something worth investigating or if it was all part of being newly married. Angie finally decided something was wrong when, after a fight, Todd went to the den, shut the door, and told Angie to "leave him alone." Angie stood at the door trying to figure out what to do when she heard explicit noises coming from the room and the computer. Angie opened the door and found Todd engaged in pornography. Todd, embarrassed and ashamed, explained he had been using pornography long before they were married. He said he had planned on stopping once they were married, thought that being married would solve it because he would "finally be able to actually have sex." But their honeymoon had been such a disaster that he had started using pornography again as a way to deal with the difficulty in their marriage. Todd knew he needed help but was too embarrassed to do anything about it. Angie, never having dealt with anything like this before, didn't know what to do either.

There Is Nothing Rational about Pornography

Our neo-cortex—the front part of our brain—is responsible for our rational thinking. It is the part of the brain that we use to think about whether we are going to buy a red shirt or a blue one, whether our spouse was right or wrong, or what steps we need to take to mend our relationship. Pornography damages this functional, rational part of our brain.

The limbic part of the brain is our reptilian brain. This means that more of our basic survival instincts are located here. Our "fight or flight" response is found here as well as our fear responses. When stimulated with enough pornography, the limbic system becomes the dominant structure in the brain as opposed to our neo-cortex. The rational is then replaced by the irrational.

When those who view pornography are faced with a conflict, stress, or negative emotions within their relationships, their limbic brain believes that those emotions are too overwhelming to handle. It then takes over and triggers an addictive response. Rather than dealing with the emotions rationally, addicted individuals turn to pornography to help alleviate those emotions. This same process can create migraines, body pains, chronic illnesses, anger, poor impulse control, and other non-relationship-oriented means to come to a resolution or conclusion.

In other words, when the limbic part of our brain is in charge, and our neo-cortex, or rational thought, is following behind, we engage in all sorts of self-defeating behaviors our rational mind would never condone! We literally cannot use any sort of logical thinking to resolve conflict and are stuck in "limbo" in our limbic mind.

So, How Do We Get out of "Limbo"?

Excessive TV or sports watching, web surfing, video gaming, computer gaming, and any pornography viewing are all limbic in nature. Now, we aren't saying it isn't okay or normal to want to just "veg out" sometimes. In our hurried world, it's nice to be able to "tune out" what may be bothering us for a little while and stop thinking.

However, you know you are existing more in your limbic structure if you get upset for several days if your favorite team does not win the ball game. An hour or two of upset is acceptable, but when the loss disrupts your job and family life, you are far too much in your limbic structures. It's time for an attitude adjustment and a reality check.

Start paying attention to how much time you are actually spending on these types of activities and see if there are other, more real activities you could engage in instead, such as going for a walk, gardening, conversing, and so on.

This Goes All the Way Down to Our Chemicals . . .

There are a variety of chemicals activated in both men and women during sexual activity. The chemicals listed below play the most dominant role and greatly affect our experience and bonding. Like anything else, they can be used to enhance our relationship with one another, or, unfortunately, enhance our dysfunction and isolation.

The "Rush" of a Relationship or the "Fear" of One

Adrenaline and epinephrine are present when we are engaged in sexual activity with our spouse. We feel that rush and explosion of emotion and passion. It's exciting and we literally can feel "turned on" due to the effects of those two chemicals.

When we are involved with pornography, we are involved with an object, and our brain knows it. Our brain knows we are not truly interacting with another living human being. That being said, our body still reacts and still emits these chemicals, but in different ways, using them to enhance fabricated pleasure and fabricated bonding.

You see, viewing images of unclothed women or men triggers a fear, fight, or flight response, which quickens the heartbeat and increases the skin temperature, and we become flooded with these exciting, rush-filled chemicals. Each time we then revisit these experiences in our mind, we also reexperience the chemical wash through the fantasy of what we just viewed on our mind's stage.

Basically, we get that rush from an object or image in our own mind, without having to interact with anyone! So why bother when we can get that same feeling without the potential difficulty of dealing with another living person! Instant gratification!

Creating the Ties That Bind

We have mentioned the many benefits and feel good effects of oxytocin through this book. It is the chemical present when we pick up a new puppy, share a hug, or have positive touch. It is the chemical bond between a man or woman. The greatest amount of oxytocin and vasopressin emitted by women takes place when she is giving birth to a child. This chemical experience between mother and child is lifelong and cements the bonding between these two individuals into eternity.

A man also feels these chemicals when bonding to his wife and children, yet they are most present in a man when he is having an ejaculation—with or without intercourse. Think of this dynamic: What if a man is ejaculating to a pornographic image? He then is creating a chemical bond to whatever it is he is viewing.

It's a dysfunctional chemical connection, but it is occurring nonetheless. It's simple cause and effect, only these effects are harmful instead of helpful. Can you begin to see the confusion and desperation of the brain as it finds itself bonded to a non-reality photo or video that never talks and where it cannot have a real relationship? However, can you also see how the brain would start to want more of the non-reality—it's easier than dealing with everyday reality instead.

This begins to explain the consequence of unleashing these chemicals through pornography. We cannot escape the consequences; they are fixed, real, and tragic. We get to choose whether we engage in pornography; we don't get to choose the consequences of our choice no matter how much we want to think we "control" our level of involvement.

We Are Creatures of Habit—for Good or for Bad

In a fireside, Carlos Asay says we are a "walking bundle of habits." C.A. Hill expands on that idea by saying, "We sow our thoughts, and we reap our actions; we sow our actions, and we reap our habits; we sow our habits, and we reap our characters; we sow our characters, and we reap our destiny." As therapists, we have seen the unfortunate consequences time after time for those who are addicted and those who are on the other side of an addiction. We see people who have lost jobs, family, and self-worth—due to the slavery of their addiction.

The scriptures clearly state how Satan presents dangerous and life-altering scenarios as seemingly harmless pursuits:

He leadeth them by the neck with a flaxen cord, until he bindeth them with his strong cords forever. (2 Nephi 26:22)

For behold, at that day shall [the devil] rage in the hearts of the children of men, and stir them up to anger against that which is good. And others will he pacify, and lull them away into carnal security . . . And thus the devil cheateth their souls, and leadeth them away carefully down to hell. (Nephi 28:20-21)

And he beheld Satan; and he had a great chain in his hand, and it veiled the whole face of the earth with darkness; and he looked up and laughed, and his angels rejoiced. (Moses 7:26)

Broadening The Definition

Pornography ultimately steals the hearts of "men" away from their spouses and families and gives an unrealistic impression of what sex is. We have seen a similar phenomenon with women—and some men— who get caught in the trap of steamy romance novels, movies, and relationship reality shows. Relationships are depicted in a fantasy-type setting: we are not shown the lulls, arguments, the communication glitches, morning breath, and authentic human interactions. We are merely being shown the "highlights" or edited version of a relationship. These movies, shows, and novels have the ability to pull your heart away from your spouse, painting unrealistic expectations that cannot be met unless you were married to a "Stepford" wife or husband. The authors tell the story with the intent to create an over-the-top romance, a fairy tale fantasy, editing out anything that is real or detracts from a happy ending. When this starts feeling better than our reality, it creates frustration, distance, and thoughts about our spouse's inadequacies. It moves into a destructive and harmful realm like pornography—just less noticeable and overtly harmful. Pornography is not limited to overtly sexual images. It's anything that distorts your perception of reality and pulls your heart away from whom it is committed to. It can be equally alluring and damaging to a relationship.

Pornographic addiction happens slowly over time, experience by experience. It subtly lures you into its web and away from the things that matter most in this life. Satan, the author of lies and deceit, gets pornography users to lie to themselves about not viewing it "all that much" and being able to "stop at any time."

The truth is, by the time you realize you have a problem, you are usually in deeper than you think. Again, Satan loves to show up at this point to plant seeds of doubt in your ability to get out and to negate the truth of the Savior's Atonement in your life.

Hope and Recovery

Considering how pornography affects your brain and chemicals, can one overcome the ravages and chains of pornography and return to a true intimate relationship? The answer is, "Yes!" The Atonement is powerful, real, and accessible.

In Romans, we are given a great message of hope:

> Therefore being justified by faith, we have peace with God through our Lord Jesus Christ: By whom also we have access by faith into this grace wherein we stand, and rejoice in the hope of the glory of God. And not only so, but we glory in tribulations also: knowing that tribulation worketh patience and patience, experience; and experience, hope: And hope maketh not ashamed; because of the love of God is shed abroad in our hearts by the Holy Ghost which is given unto us. (Romans 5:1–5)

These verses speak of Heavenly Father, Jesus Christ, and the Holy Ghost being with us to help us through our difficult times. They clearly state that although we will experience "tribulations," these things will give us "patience," "experience" and, eventually, "hope." Those things aren't obtained easily but are obtainable. It will take commitment and hard work. Through Christ, who is the Great Counselor and giver of hope, healing and recovery are possible. Another beautiful gift from this scripture is the opportunity to address and let go of shame by feeling this same hope.

Taking the necessary steps to move toward recovery can feel daunting and scary. Yet the Lord will fill in the emotional, physical, and spiritual gaps. In Isaiah 58:11 it reads:

"And the Lord shall guide thee continually, and satisfy thy soul in drought, and make fat thy bones: and thou shalt be like a watered garden, and like a spring of water, whose waters fail not."

Recovery requires a commitment to major lifestyle changes, new skills, self-understanding, ecclesiastical intervention, and hours of individual and group therapy. Both types of therapy are necessary to return pornography-addicted individuals from this devastating lifestyle.

You must become as the "little child" mentioned in the scriptures—humble, submissive, and willing in all things. Recovery from an addiction to pornography is only possible with complete disclosure, total abstinence, and transparency into all aspects of your life. No doubt the hardest step will be the first one, but it will be the first toward getting your life back.

Angie and Todd Continued . . .

After Todd disclosed his addiction to Angie, she felt angry, scared, and embarrassed. She didn't know what to do. Todd, as well, was feeling alone, hopeless, and ashamed. After praying and taking some time to think about what they wanted, they decided to seek help individually and as a couple. Angie and Todd loved each other for many reasons and wanted to see if they could still make their marriage work. They knew it would take a huge amount of commitment, time, patience, forgiveness, and work.

At first, the "mountain" in front of them seemed overwhelming and impossible to climb. However, with time and perspective, they began to see the progress they were making. They were still unsure about the future, but they had the hope that together with the Lord and with other supporters, they would climb that jagged peak and feel the healing warmth of the sun on their faces.

REAL RELATIONSHIP TIP!
Keeping Our Relationship Agency in Place

By comparing how God and Jesus approach relationships versus Satan, we can better apply the healthy model to our lives and avoid Satan's relationship "advice." Satan would like us to believe that pornography will not harm anybody or our relationship. But ultimately it takes us down a path where we forgo our choice and our agency and are in throes of an addiction. In the neo-cortex—the brain's rational center—there is always choice involved. "Thou mayest choose for

---

thyself, for it is given unto thee"(Moses 3:17).

SATAN	THE FATHER AND THE SON
He always comes alone (Moses 1:12)	They always come together (JS History 1:17)
Control (Alma 12:17)	Free choice (Helaman 14:30)
Works of darkness (2 Nephi 26:22)	Good works
Me-oriented	We-oriented (Moses 4:2)
The counterfeit and illusion (Alma 12:6)	The real thing: men, women and children
Will not support us; will only drag us down (Alma 30:60)	He stands up for us (John 8:3–8)
Pleasure	Joy, growth, eternal learning
Non-relationship	Relationship
My needs	The needs of others
Death is the end; guaranteed gratification (Alma 30:16–18)	Eternal perspective
It's not fair	His ways are just (D&C 93:20)
Entitlement; you deserve it	Sacrifice brings forth the blessings of Heaven
Nothing you do matters (Alma 30:17)	All things affect the outcome (D&C 81:6)
You're not hurting anyone else	Maintenance of the Spirit
Doesn't care about us; is inherently selfish	Sacrificed for us because He loves us (D&C 50:41)
It won't matter	It always matters (D&C 50:43–45)
No one will ever know	All things are known
No resolve	Resolve (D&C 10:5)

THE NUTS AND BOLTS

Pornography is the greatest mental health and social problem in the religious life and community of our generation.

That may seem like an exaggeration, but, unfortunately, it's not. Attention must be paid to this subject. If you think that because you don't have an addiction to pornography and that it's not affecting you or your relationship, you are wrong. Pornography is everywhere. There's hardly a person who hasn't viewed, intentionally or not, some sort of pornography—on TV, at the movies, or on the Internet. Those images are instantly recalled—forever. There is a reason for this, which this chapter covered. This is the reality of pornography, and you must pay attention.

Pornography's greatest lie is that it provides guaranteed gratification every time we open it, look at it, read it, or allow a past visualization or sexual scenario to cross our minds. There is almost nothing in existence that can make that same claim. Pornography does not require our full attention, our money, a clean shave, or a brushed and bathed person—we can receive instant gratification even if we have not showered in two weeks. It doesn't talk back. It demands nothing of us. It never requires a relationship. We don't have to talk to it or show any intelligence to obtain or use it. We don't even have to leave our homes to download it, abuse it and receive gratification from it day or night.

Pornography greatly impacts our brain and the chemicals in our brain. This chapter described how our thinking becomes distorted.

Recovery requires a commitment to major lifestyle changes, new skills, self-understanding, ecclesiastical intervention, and hours of individual and group therapy. Both types of therapy are needed to return pornography-addicted individuals from this devastating lifestyle. You must become as the "little child" mentioned in the scriptures—humble, submissive, and willing in all things. Recovery from an addiction to pornography is only possible with complete disclosure, total abstinence, and with transparency. No doubt the hardest step will be the first one—but it will be the first toward getting your life back.

Chapter Questions for Real-Life Application

1. Has pornography impacted your relationship? If so, how? Is there anything you need to change?

2. If someone you love is involved with pornography, what are you

doing to not only support them, but also support yourself as well? There are many resources available for those addicted to pornography—as well as spouses impacted.

3. Spend some time finding and reading scriptures on hope and healing. The Great Counselor is always available—even when your earthly counselor is not.

16

MILLENNIAL INTIMACY
Twenty-first-century challenges and connections

C AN YOU REMEMBER NOT HAVING A CELL PHONE? CAN YOU remember the first dial-up Internet connections and how long it would take for one page to load, if you could even get on in the first place? Thanks to social media, Generation X—or those between the ages of thirty and fifty—is now the most socially connected generation in history! And who knows just how connected future generations will be. We're now keeping up with the friends we had when we were three years old! We move at a faster pace, gobble an incredible amount of information, and juggle more and more balls. If you don't think this has an impact on your intimacy or your ability to be intimate, think again. Welcome to the twenty-first century!

Technology is not going to go away, and we wouldn't want it to. We can communicate with far more people than ever before, and, usually, be more productive. Ask military spouses how grateful they are to actually see their loved one, via the Internet, half a world away. But like the various aspects of intimacy we have discussed in this book so far, the key is finding balance and the best ways to use technology so it enhances rather than undermines our most important relationships. Understanding how it affects us and the people in our lives will help us maintain the actual relationships we do have and bring them into the twenty-first century.

With cell phones, smart phones, and tablets, media is finding its way into our lives at an ever-increasing rate. Now a quiet dinner with your spouse can be interrupted by people calling, texting, or tweeting. Pre-9/11, you could walk down a street and actually make eye contact with people. Occasionally, you would actually make a potential date in person as opposed to texting or "Facebooking" them. As we become more wired and connected via computers, we are becoming less intimate and personal as people. Often some of the relationships we consider to be our closest are now with people we have never in met in person! The key is finding balance and setting boundaries. Technology continues to find more ways to reduce privacy and increase our public information. It's up to us to set our boundaries, find our balance, and use technology in a wise way so that it enhances our life instead of taking away from it.

Cell Phones and Texting

Cell phones have become such a mainstream part of our culture that it's almost unheard of to find someone who doesn't have one. Kids as young as six are being handed phones in case they need to call their parents. This has changed the way we communicate. If we can't get ahold of someone immediately, we wonder why. Gone are the days of "busy signals"—we leave a voicemail or send a text. Smart phones become a problem when we can't leave them alone, even for a few minutes, in order to have an actual conversation with our spouse, friend, or child.

Recently there was a Christmas card going around that spoofed society's growing addiction to cell phones. A family was posed in a traditional way, but each member was looking at a smart phone or tablet. While the truth of this is sad, the reality is, it is funny to most of us because we can all relate. We can identify with being physically in the same area as someone yet be in an entirely different world dominated by an illuminated screen. Consider the couple who decides to watch a movie together but instead of cuddling, they share a blanket and cuddle their phones. Again, simply being physically present in the same room is not the same as bringing your presence to the room.

Craig

Craig noticed cell phones were becoming a problem in his home, especially with his teenage children, and therefore instituted a "no cell phones after 8:00 p.m." rule. He said it was difficult at first, but now he and his family spend more time together in the evenings, and he and his wife now have more time to unwind from the day if they are able to "unplug" together.

Texting is another animal altogether. Texting has its own lingo and some English language purists are worried texting is ruining teens' abilities to complete a sentence, spell, or have correct grammar! Unfortunately, texting is also making it more difficult to actually speak to one another.

Bailey and Logan

Bailey met Logan at the gym and they exchanged numbers. Instead of talking, they spent quite a bit of time texting. Logan asked Bailey out through text. Their date was awkward because although they had revealed much of their inner life in texts, they didn't know how to bridge that into an actual conversation. After a few dates, Bailey decided to end the relationship—by a text.

What do you think their next possible relationship would be like? If this is the primary way Bailey and Logan interact with others, they may find themselves wondering why they are spending so much time alone! Now that texting has been around for awhile, we are starting to see the effects of too much instant messaging. People are having a difficult time actually initiating a live conversation and then knowing what to do from there. Of course, it's not as scary to ask someone out on a date through text, but it's also far less personable. Get your relationship started right by cultivating the communication between you and your partner from the beginning.

On the other hand, texting can be a wonderful way to send a quick message like, "I love you" or "Just leaving"; but sending angry texts can be damaging. One of the biggest negatives of texting is you only get minimal information and condensed content. You miss the facial expressions, body language, voice tone, or opportunity to really explain yourself. We often say things in text that we would never say in person. Again, texting can be a great way to send a quick "I love you" message, coordinate plans, or message of encouragement. But if you haven't actually spoken those words to your partner in awhile, it's time. There is no substitute for human interaction.

"Sexting" is another big issue with texting. "Sexting" is the term used to describe the sending of revealing pictures through text. Take into consideration how both of you feel about this. It would be no different than other aspects of sexuality you are not comfortable with. Also, if you are going to send your husband a picture of your cleavage, you might want to make sure he's not in the middle of a church meeting! Just remember, whatever you send out in the virtual world, you almost never can take it back. Another consideration is once you put information into "the cloud," you relinquish control of how it is used, who sees it, and for what purposes it is used. While this could be fun for a husband and wife, it is not appropriate in any other realm.

Blogs and Social Media

More people are having the opportunity to try their hand at being journalists or writers through blogs and social media. There are general family blogs, topic-specific blogs, or blogs dedicated to making individuals and communities more aware. Again, it's great to stay in touch with people we wouldn't otherwise be able to by reading their blogs. However, we are hearing from people that self-esteem drops as they compare themselves to these "super people." In fact one client said she committed "Internet suicide" when she deleted her blog permanently. One thing about blogs and social media is the authors also get to be the editors and post only the things they want in order to be seen in a positive way.

If you are spending your time reading things that are not "virtuous, lovely, or of good report or praiseworthy" (which can mean it simply doesn't make you feel good), it can take a toll on your intimacy and your relationship because it's impacting how you feel about yourself or how you are seeing the world around you. It can also take a toll on how you view your spouse if you are reading about all of the things other romantic husbands and wives are doing for each other. The truth is, we stack our perceived weaknesses and our spouse's against the strength of others. Additionally, we take a blogged-about idyllic moment and assume their relationship is like that every day. We counsel our clients to consider taking a break from social media sites or blogs that are not uplifting or make you feel "less than."

REAL RELATIONSHIP TIP!
How Facebook Can Complement Your Marriage

Facebook is shaping how 120 million people stay in touch with their friends, family, coworkers, and acquaintances. Here are five practical ways to improve your relationship through Facebook.

(1) Set Your Status to Married—While this seems like a no-brainer, your relationship status is one of the first pieces of information other people view. Your relationship status acts like a wedding ring on your hand and will likely influence how some of your FB friends interact with you.

(2) Get Married to Your Spouse on Facebook—If your spouse is on Facebook, link your profiles together by identifying each other as the person you are married to. A message goes out to everyone in your network that you are "now married." Get ready for a flurry of comments such as, "finally!" or "it's about time!" Being married on Facebook makes it easier to view each other's updates and profiles, and to communicate with one another through Facebook messages and chat.

(3) Affirm Your Marriage & Mate Often—Let the world (or at least your social network) hear about your spouse through status updates and wall posts. Proclaim your love for your spouse and what he/she does for you as a regular part of your updates. Just this week, several FB friends posted the following comments in their status update: "I'm madly in love with my wife," "I'm so proud of my husband for closing two deals this week," and "I can't wait 'til my wife gets back from Texas." These kinds of messages can have a profound effect and encourage others to do the same. Every once in awhile it will spark a response like, "Sometimes these little comments are so sappy, suckuppy, sweet—they make me want to barf!" But that is more the exception than the rule. Ultimately, your spouse benefits the most because

they'll receive another reminder that they are loved.

(4) Connect with Your Mate through Facebook—Chatting and messaging through Facebook is a great way to keep connected with your spouse throughout the day. It can be accessed by computer and smart phones. Couples can use this real time feature whether they're in different parts of the house, different parts of town, or different parts of the world. We have a FB friend who travels the world and uses Facebook and Skype to keep in touch with his wife. Use Facebook chat to share quick updates, give a reminder of the day's to-do list, or flirt with one another. Chat sessions permanently erase upon logging off so "what happens on Facebook stays on Facebook."

(5) Keep Your Spouse Updated in Real Time—Take face-to-face time to talk about your Facebook networks. You likely have a number of common FB friends in your networks, but you also have people from your past or present that your spouse doesn't know personally. Share about new FB friends, new connections, funny or informative posts you read that day. Technology is there to complement day-to-day communication, not replace it.

Used with permission by K. Jason and Kelli Krafsky from their website: www.fbmarriage.com

Gaming

Another area of technology that has adversely impacted relationships is gaming—video games, traditional home-gaming devices, and games found on the Internet or social media sites. These virtual worlds can be alluring because players have complete control over them, receive large amounts of praise and reward, and are surrounded by other people who have the same interests. While gaming can be a nice hobby or even a way to relax or escape, the issue of appropriate balance comes up again. If you find you are spending more time building up your virtual "farm" or leading your virtual "army" than you are with your real family and real relationship, it's time to re-evaluate. Gaming can turn into a way to numb the stresses of your life and relationship. If not used in moderation, your virtual relationships can easily become the primary relationships you are nurturing and with whom you are giving your best time and attention.

Internet Dating

In our fast-paced, migratory world, some people have found it difficult to meet potential mates the old-fashioned way and have turned to various social media sites. There are highly publicized success stories that have encouraged more people to try this method. The trick is taking your virtual relationship and turning it into a real relationship. It's easy to become personal when you're not face-to-face and having to deal with the immediate emotions or reactions of the other person. Also, we can be whoever we want in the virtual world—becoming the person we hope to be instead of the person we are. This deception causes us to split from the reality of ourselves and makes it more difficult to be "real" with the other person as well!

Frank and Julie

Frank and Julie began emailing each other after responding to a profile on a social media site. They shared their hopes, dreams, goals, pains, and losses. After three weeks of emailing, they decided to get married. When Julie met Frank for the first time, he didn't quite seem like the man she had been writing but decided to move forward with their plans. After five painful months of marriage, Julie discovered Frank was extremely involved with pornography as well as other women over the Internet. Frank admitted he liked his Internet persona better than his real one and sometimes couldn't even distinguish between real Frank and virtual Frank. He and Julie divorced soon after, and Frank returned to his virtual relationships, where he didn't have to deal with a real person with real emotions, real needs, real weaknesses, and even a real body. There must be a balance between what you are experiencing on the Internet and what you are experiencing in reality. If the majority of your time is spent with online relationships, then you need to rethink your priorities.

Internet Infidelity

This is dangerously easy. It's too easy to look up an old boyfriend or girlfriend on the Internet in the hopes of rekindling something when maybe things in your marriage aren't great. When we remember those relationships, we generally recall only the happy times, which we then unfairly compare to the bad times in our marriage! "Well, so-and-so would always bring me flowers when I had a bad day! Why doesn't my husband?" "I wonder what so-and-so is doing now? I'll just do a quick search and find out. My husband won't even have to know and I'm not really hurting anybody anyway!" So, you do a search a find him. Then what? Do you contact him? What if he's married? What if she's not? Social media sites like Facebook have made it easy to find and contact people in the secrecy of our own homes. You might never consider having lunch with an old girlfriend, but you could easily send her a quick message just to see how she is doing. This is dangerous territory and you must be careful. A few seemingly innocent conversations can lead to intimate discussions. Then you find you are looking forward to those messages more than conversations with your spouse! Did you see it? Did you see the line? At what point did it cross into emotional infidelity? The Internet has made what was once a black-and-white issue gray.

Janna and Brett

Janna ran into an old boyfriend, Brett, at the store. He was there with his kids, and she with hers. She was excited to see him, and some old feelings came rushing back. In the five minutes they took to catch up, he shared with her that he was getting divorced due to his wife's infidelity. Janna said she was on Facebook and would look him up in order to give him more support during this difficult time. The ex-boyfriend beat Janna to the punch by finding her first, but he did something both she and her husband appreciated—to whom Janna had disclosed her conversation. Brett requested both Janna and her husband as "friends" in order to maintain complete transparency and also to respect Janna's marriage.

It is possible to be unfaithful to your spouse without ever leaving the confines of your own home. Remember the movie *You've Got Mail*? The two characters in that movie developed quite an emotional connection over email. Both characters were already in committed relationships, but drifted away from those as their email relationship became more and more involved. However, in real life, the two characters actually despised one another, not having any idea they were actually communicating with each other over the Internet! While this plot made for a cute, romantic comedy—and we're not trying to ruin this movie for any of you who love it—the reality of the situation displays the danger of Internet infidelity.

Both characters were their "best" selves over email, and consoled the other over whatever might have been lacking in their current relationship. Had they known with whom they were communicating, both of them would have completely backed away. In fact, at one point in the movie, the male character discovers with whom he has been communicating and almost can't handle it. The movie ends with the two of them discovering the truth of the situation and with them walking off into the proverbial sunset together. The audience doesn't get to see them try to resolve the Internet personas versus the actual flesh-and-blood people. The audience just assumes everybody lives "happily ever after."

If you are finding yourself spending a lot of time emailing, messaging, video chatting, and so on, with someone other than your spouse, you are crossing into the danger zone. It would be time to take a step back and ask yourself a few questions:

1) Would you be having this conversation in front of your spouse?

2) Would you feel comfortable with your spouse knowing about your online relationship?

3) How would you feel if your spouse were having conversations like this with another person?

If you wouldn't be okay with your spouse reading any of the emails or knowing about your online relationship, then you have definitely crossed over and need to step back. Your relationship is probably worth fighting for. Take the energy you were putting into your virtual relationship and put it back into your real one.

Technology Is Like the "Condiments"

If intimacy is the main dish, appetizer, or dessert, than technology could be the condiments. Condiments should enhance "the meat and potatoes" not *be* the meat and potatoes. Can you imagine filling up on ketchup packets? I'm sure the pioneers would have loved to communicate some logistical information as they were crossing the plains, or send a, "Good job, Honey!" while they were a few hand-carts away. But having our intimacy balance start to tilt toward mostly being in the form of "millennial intimacy" you may find your relationship becoming increasingly malnourished. Using technology as it was intended—to enhance rather than distract—can bring fun, connection, and love to your relationship.

We have at our fingertips an incredible amount of power and knowledge. Everything God puts on this earth can be used to further His plan and make our lives better—including technology. We can use technology to add flavor and spice to our relationship. We can download podcasts that may educate on how to enhance our marriage. We can spend less time paying bills or other mundane tasks, giving us more time with each other. We can pick the perfect restaurant, order flowers, and send cute messages throughout the day, thanks to technology.

Tim and Karen

Tim and Karen had busy lives. They both worked and had four children. They had little time to plan dates or even just be together. Karen decided to add a little spice to her day and connect with her husband in a way she wouldn't connect with anybody else during the day. She sent him a few intimate texts and emails. Tim thought they were great and would respond in kind. They both felt like they shared a stronger connection during the day and looked even more forward to being together at night. Karen also said it helped her be more focused on Tim during her hectic day with kids and work, which allowed her to transition to being physically intimate with him.

THE NUTS AND BOLTS

No, "Millennial Intimacy" is not referring to intimacy during the Millennium. It is, however, referring to the challenges and benefits of our twenty-first-century technology and how it impacts our relationships. Basically, think about how often you use the following:

TV

Cell phones

Social media

Internet

Gaming systems

All these wonderful inventions can negatively impact our personal relationships if we are using them to replace, avoid, or ignore the actual human beings in our lives. Not only will our time be greatly divided but our emotional and mental capacity to interact as well. It's important to take a personal inventory of the time and energy you are putting into technology and make adjustments if necessary. For example, you may need to set aside your nightly "surfing" and spend that time with your spouse instead.

Use texting to send your spouse a quick, loving message. Use Facebook to keep up with family members. Use video chat to talk to your spouse the next time you are out of town. The positive ways to utilize technology are endless—it just takes a little bit of extra effort on your part.

If you find spend a lot of time emailing, messaging, video chatting, and so on, with someone than your spouse, you are crossing into a danger zone. Internet infidelity is becoming more prevalent as we are able to connect with ex-girlfriends, coworkers, or someone who just seems to "appreciate us" in a way our spouse just doesn't. If you relate to any of those scenarios, it's time to take a step back and ask yourself a few questions:

(1) Would you be having this conversation in front of your spouse?

(2) Would you feel comfortable with your spouse knowing about your online relationship?

(3) How would you feel if your spouse were having conversations like this with another person?

(4) If you answered no to the first two questions and "wouldn't like it" to the third, then you need to step back over the line and come back to your real relationship. More than likely it's worth fighting for.

Chapter Questions for Real-Life Application

1. Keep a seven-day record of how much time you spend watching TV, talking on the phone, texting, surfing, gaming, and so on.

Compare that to the amount of time you spend interacting with your spouse or children. Do you need to make an adjustment?

2. Are there any online relationships that have crossed into the danger zone?

3. Send your spouse a nice text, email, or voicemail each day for a week. Notice how, or if, this impacts your relationship.

4. Do you find yourself looking forward to spending time on your "farm" or with your virtual friends more than your spouse or children? If so, spend some time thinking about what you are getting out of these online experiences that you feel are lacking from your "real" life. Discuss this with your spouse.

17

THE PHYSICAL BODY AND SEX

How our diet, weight, hygiene habits, and substance use and abuse affect our sexuality

WE HOPE YOU HAVE LEARNED THAT INTIMACY AND SEX ARE dynamic, multifaceted experiences. The reality is there are few things about intimacy that are simple, straightforward, and not without caveats. The same holds true for our physical body. Our bodies do amazing things. Some go unnoticed, like battling an invading bacterium. We see the results, but we don't see what is really happening.

As it relates to sex, there is a lot happening physiologically, intellectually, and emotionally with our bodies. Some things we can see and others are actively happening behind the scenes. You may have discovered new things about yourself in the "Understanding Your Libido" chapter when we talked about the libido spectrum. Our hope is to give you information about the body so you can better understand about yourself, your partner, and different elements impacting your sexuality. While we are not going into a lot of detail, this information should give you a starting point to determine if what you are experiencing is a medical, emotional, or circumstantial issue. Remember, every "body" is different and responds to things in unique ways. If you find yourself potentially dealing with something in this chapter that is disruptive to you or your relationship, seek out the opinion of a medical professional or a mental health therapist.

Hygiene

It's said that "cleanliness is next to Godliness." A regular shower, a bar of soap, a toothbrush, and a stick of deodorant can be your best friend when it comes to intimacy. After you shower, make sure you are completely dry before getting dressed to avoid creating a breeding ground for odor-causing bacteria. Pay particular attention to drying under your arms and your genitals. Be sure to wash your hands regularly to avoid passing germs.

Women should take regular baths or showers and wash the outside of your vagina with mild soap; your body will do the rest to keep your vagina clean. Using scented tampons, pad, sprays, douches, or powders can increase your chances of getting a vaginal infection. Douches actually interfere with the natural mucous that is created to clean blood, semen, and discharge. If you are experiencing strong odor due to discharge; yellow, thick, or greenish discharge with or without an odor; or pain during sex or when you urinate, see your doctor to be treated for a potential medical condition.

Men, if you are uncircumcised, take special consideration to wash under your foreskin. Additionally, men emit a chemical found in their natural sweat that brings out sexual desire in women. If you are not keeping yourself clean, you can block this natural scent!

For both men and women, it's normal for your genitalia, regardless of how clean it is, to have a natural mild odor.

Medication

Many prescribed or over-the-counter medications cause side effects that can impact your sexual functioning. They can show up immediately or over time. Prior to taking any medication, consult with your doctor about both the potential short- and long-term side effects.

REAL RELATIONSHIP TIP!
Did You Know?

- Did you know you can increase your "feel good" chemicals by giving or receiving a thirty-second hug? Feeling good decreases levels of cortisol that are responsible for stress. That's not only a

heart that's happy, that's a heart that's healthy!
- Did you know during a passionate kiss, you can actually burn two calories a minute? Compare that with eleven calories a minute on a treadmill.
- Did you know that saliva contains testosterone that affects your sexual motivation? Next time you need a desire boost, start with a kiss!

Greg

After returning from his second tour of duty in Afghanistan, Greg began taking antidepressants to help him deal with his experiences. He was frustrated with what he considered to be a "weakness" and was having trouble dealing with the changes in his life. He began experiencing trouble achieving and maintaining an erection during sex. At first Greg attributed this to his new sense of "weakness" and withdrew from his wife. However, the next time he spoke with his doctor, he decided to mention what was happening to make sure his "body wasn't falling apart" as a result of his time overseas. The doctor immediately eased Greg's concerns explaining to Greg about the possible side effects of antidepressants—one of them being difficulty in achieving and maintaining erections. This gave Greg new perspective, and he had his medication adjusted.

Body Image

Discontentment with body image is not only an issue for women. Many men report dissatisfaction in the way they feel about their body. A negative body image—whether it's how you view yourself or feel that others view your body—can contribute to a low self-esteem, reduce confidence, influence the decisions we make, and create anxiety surrounding sexuality and our "sexiness." We live in a society that sells the idea that one type of body is the ideal and what ultimately makes us happy. Remember our section on Hollywood and all of the messages we received about sex and intimacy? We get the same polluted messages about our bodies. Often our expectations and views of ourselves are unrealistic, which causes us to be unfairly critical of our bodies. Women, can you relate to this after you've had a baby? You may be surprised to hear how your spouse views your body and loves all of you. Increase your self-awareness with the critical messages you tell yourself. You may also have messages that you heard and internalized growing up or from other people. We often say things to ourselves or hold on to messages we would never say to another human being. If you have difficulty overcoming these thoughts, or if a negative body image is getting in the way of a healthy relationship with your spouse, consider getting outside help.

Weight

Obesity takes a toll on many aspects of the body. It contributes to heart disease, bad circulation (see the importance of blood flow and the body in diets and exercise), depression, low self-esteem, diabetes, reduced muscular function, and other issues which impact sexuality. In men, excessive weight can increase the chances of developing Erectile Dysfunction by 30 percent. Women are four times more likely to have an unplanned pregnancy and are at higher risk for complications during pregnancy than healthy weight individuals. By creating a reasonable weight-control plan with your doctor, you will improve your health, intimacy, and sexual life.

Diet and Exercise

In her book *The Better Sex Diet*, Lynn Fischer says that by eating a diet that improves the health of your heart, you increase the blood flow to other organs in your body. As we learned in the Sex Ed 101 chapter, both men's and women's sexual arousal and orgasm are dependent on adequate blood flow to the genitals. If your diet has excessive amounts of sugar, caffeine, high-fat content, or processed chemicals you can suppress your body's ability to function at its best. Eating balanced meals can improve your sexual desire and performance.

Substance Abuse

Drugs, including prescription medication, alcohol, or illegal substances affect our body. The two major areas that are affected are desire and sexual functioning. Substances impact capillaries that deliver blood to the genitals, which allow for erections to occur and be sustained, and help facilitate natural lubrication in women. Our sexual desire can be suppressed and our hormones altered.

Lisa

Lisa experienced a major car accident after she was married. She suffered back and neck injuries that required pain medication. Soon Lisa began using her pain medication continually and felt a need for larger doses to maintain a feeling of "normalcy." However, what Lisa didn't anticipate was an almost complete drop in her desire for sex with her husband as well as difficulty in achieving orgasm. Lisa decided this was due to her injuries and continued taking her pain medication.

Sexual Disorders and Dysfunctions

According to the DSM-IV, the manual used to diagnose mental health issues, there are approximately ten sexual disorders that both men and women can experience. Though these disorders show up in a physical way, often they have an emotional root cause such as intimacy and relationship issues, sexual abuse, rape, fear, anxiety, reactions to prescribed medications, or substance abuse. It's important to note that everyone can experience these symptoms at various times in their life depending on age and life circumstances. They are not considered disorders or dysfunctional. However, if any of the following listed happen frequently or cause significant distress in you or your relationship, we recommend seeking professional help.

Female

Female Orgasmic Disorder—The inability of a woman to have an orgasm. This can be related to intimacy issues, fear or anxiety, or not feeling safe or secure in the relationship or in relationships in general.

Female Sexual Arousal Disorder—When a woman is unable to create or maintain adequate lubrication while having sex. *Note: If you are breast feeding or are perimenopausal or menopausal, you can have difficulty creating natural lubrication due to the low levels of estrogen and the high levels of progesterone.*

Vaginismus—When a woman's vagina frequently and involuntarily spasms and causes significant distress. This can manifest in women who grew up in a strict religious home, have intense feelings about control, or have had experiences of sexual abuse or rape.

Male

Male Erectile Disorder (ED)—Being unable to achieve or maintain an erection. Also known as impotence, ED first must be treated by ruling out an underlying medical issue. If no medical cause is identified, this can be the result of anxiety surrounding performance.

Male Orgasmic Disorder—A delay or complete absence of an orgasm after typical levels of excitement or sexual activity. Once medical causes are ruled out, this can be the result of an association of sex with a negative life experience and typically first occurs during adolescence or young adulthood.

Premature Ejaculation—When a man ejaculates or discharges semen before, or shortly after, beginning sexual activity. Causes can be related to relationship stress, inexperience, or the newness of a relationship, issues surrounding intimacy, and control or anxiety issues.

Male and Female

Sexual Aversion Disorder—Present in both men and women, it is a strong aversion to or a complete avoidance of sexual activity. This can be due to relationship issues or a history of sexual trauma or abuse.

Dyspareunia—When a man or woman experiences persistent pain during sex. This may be related to vaginismus, or if you have a history of sexual abuse or rape.

Hypoactive Sexual Desire Disorder—When a man or woman has little to no desire to have any type of sexual activity. This could be due to relationship difficulties, large amounts of stress, or a history or sexual abuse or rape.

If you are looking for more in-depth information on these issues, please visit our resource section for recommended resources. This information is not intended to serve as a diagnoses or to replace medical or professional help.

THE NUTS AND BOLTS

We hope you have learned that intimacy and sex are dynamic, multifaceted experiences. The reality is there are few things about intimacy that are simple, straightforward and not without caveats. The same holds true for our physical body. Our bodies do amazing things—some that we are aware of and some that go unnoticed, like battling an invading bacterium. We see the results, but we don't see what is really happening.

As it relates to sex, there is a lot happening physiologically, intellectually, and emotionally with our bodies. Some things we can see and others are actively happening behind the scenes. You may have discovered new things about yourself in our Sexual Normalcy chapter when we talked about the libido spectrums. Our hope is to give you information about the body so you can better understand yourself and your partner and different elements that can impact your sexuality. While we are not going into great depth, this information will give you a starting point to determine if what you are experiencing is a medical, emotional, or circumstantial issue. Remember, every "body" is different and responds to things in unique ways. If you find yourself potentially dealing with something in this chapter that is disruptive to you or your relationship, seek out the opinion of a medical professional or a mental health therapist.

This chapter covers some things to keep in mind as to how it may or may not be impacting your capacity and motivation for sex. These things are:

Hygiene

Medication

Body Image

Weight

Diet and Exercise

Substance Abuse

Sexual Disorders and Dysfunctions

That list, while not exhaustive, is one you will want to be familiar with. There may be some things you can do to improve or enhance your sexual relationship.

Chapter Questions for Real-Life Application

1. What new insight or fact did you learn about your physical body and sex?

2. Are there aspects of your spouse's hygiene that disrupt your desire for intimacy?

3. If you take medication, are there any side effects that impact your sexuality?

4. If you struggle with body image issues, notice how often you have negative thoughts about your body and then try to counter them with positive thoughts or images. Treat yourself as you would treat a dear friend—with kindness, compassion, understanding, and patience.

18

MORE FOOD
FOR THOUGHT

Subjects that could be their own books and
deserved some acknowledgement

MARITAL RELATIONSHIPS AND INDIVIDUAL EXPERIENCES ARE complex and have an endless array of possibilities and combinations. We couldn't begin to cover all the topics related to intimacy in a single book. However, we would be remiss if we didn't at least give a nod to these important topics because of their profound impact on those experiencing them. We give suggestions for further reading and information in our resource section.

Sex and Singlehood

We want to acknowledge that singlehood is hard! If you've never been married or if you've lost a spouse through death or divorce, there isn't a magic "off" switch to turn off your sexuality and need for affection. While you certainly can experience emotional and mental intimacy as a single person, there most likely will be that need for physical intimacy, especially because we are all made to experience pleasure and enjoy our sexuality! So how do you express and acknowledge your sexual self while honoring the law of chastity? Unfortunately, there isn't a nice tidy list of things you can "do" and "not do" trying to navigate these waters. It's not our place to determine for you your best course of action. However, as social scientists, we can present some different things to consider.

A healthy sexual relationship involves trust, communication, maturity, compromise, safety, friendship, humor, and love. Marriage is usually the safest relationship in which to experience these things—although obvious, there are exceptions. Keep in mind, marriage does not automatically provide these. However, it is through marriage or long-lasting committed relationships that many are more likely to develop these relational traits.

The power of sex and the bonds it creates are healthy and wonderful in a healthy relationship. However, they can cloud judgment when trying to decide whether to marry someone with whom you've had sex outside of marriage. Moreover, these bonds can keep you in a relationship longer than you would without the physical connection. However, rushing to get married as a solution to a high sex drive is not a healthy option either.

Find meaningful ways to make the law of chastity work to your advantage. It is intended to be a protection after all. The Church's stance on abstaining from sex outside of marriage applies to every adult regardless of circumstances. We encourage you—whether single, married, divorced, or widowed—to understand where your morals, beliefs, and actions intersect, and to make prayerful decisions that allow you to be a healthy and happy individual.

Homosexuality

If you are reading this book and torn with yourself about your own or a loved one's sexual orientation, we want to share a message of love. Natasha Helfer Parker, marriage and family therapist, responds to a man who is grappling with his sexual orientation.

> I know many people who are heterosexual and are in wonderful relationships, are in awful relationships, are happy, are miserable, are religious, are agnostic, are spiritual, are Mormon, are not. I know many people who are homosexual and are in wonderful relationships, are in awful relationships, are happy, are miserable, are religious, are agnostic, are spiritual, are Mormon, are not. Regardless of your sexual orientation, you deserve good things in

your life. Good relationships, good self-esteem, good opportunities, good religion and most of all a knowledge of the unwavering love your Heavenly Father has for you. Being gay doesn't diminish the need for love, relationship, and intimacy. Our gay brothers and lesbian sisters are not any less deserving of love, inclusiveness, a strong sense of self-worth and a feeling of belonging in this world. (Parker)

The biggest tragedy is seeing the great despair and hopelessness people feel regarding their orientation and getting to the point of considering or planning to take their own life. If you or a loved one is having thoughts of suicide, please get help immediately. You can contact 1-800-SUICIDE any time of day or night every day of the week in a completely confidential manner.

Infidelity

While no one enters into a marriage planning to stray or to confront a spouse's infidelity, it's important to know that it can be dealt with. However, it must be treated as a crisis whether it was emotional, physical, or sexual. Remember the brain and how we talked about the chemicals that trigger fight or flight, fear and adrenalin? Those responses serve to "protect" us when we are in a situation that our brain perceives as a threat. However, when we are in crisis mode, making life-changing decisions in "the moment" may ultimately be harmful. There aren't circumstances that warrant immediate action, but certainly we want to give you a context for evaluating the relationship from a long-term perspective.

Couples that have been able to overcome the pain of infidelity often exhibit some common traits:

The unfaithful spouse shows true remorse and is willing and committed to take the steps necessary to repair the relationship.

The spouse cheated-on gives himself permission and time to heal, finds a willingness and ability to forgive, and makes a conscious decision to no longer make infidelity part of every conversation.

As a couple, both are willing and committed to address potential issues that led to the infidelity in the first place.

Looking at these issues is not the same as finding reasons to justify or excuse unfaithful actions. Part of the process of recovering from infidelity is to assess the dynamics of an obvious dysfunctional relationship. Our experience is that most relationships—despite the infidelity—deserve an honest examination. Affairs tend to be a symptom of underlying problems in the relationship, not the problem itself.

If you have a spouse that is remorseful and wanting to repair the relationship, consider focusing on what the Atonement means to you, and the benefit and gift you can both experience by bringing this into your life. The Atonement doesn't just forgive the sinner but can ease the pain of the wounded heart. If you both decide to move forward, make a conscious decision to leave this behind even if you don't know exactly how to do this.

Some couples who have lived through the experience of infidelity have likened the experience to a scar that was an initially open, painful wound. However, through the commitment from both spouses to repair the wound, it was able to scar over and become less noticeable over time. Most scars can fade significantly into the background. Despite a relationship never being the same or going back to the previous "normal," a new "normal" and level of emotional and spiritual intimacy can be created—one that you create together. There is nothing more powerful then having someone at your side who accepts, chooses, and loves all of you—even your mistakes, faults, and weaknesses. Experiences like these, although extremely painful, can ultimately add to the unique beauty of your mountain landscape. Jagged cliffs and steep sides create a dramatic backdrop.

Sexual Abuse

Unfortunately, the chances are high that either you or your spouse may have experienced some form of sexual abuse as a child or youth. The statistics are still alarmingly high. We see stories of revealed sex offenders in the news far too often. If this is the case for you or your spouse, please know first and foremost—you are not alone! Often victims of sexual abuse feel significant guilt, shame, fear, mistrust, and isolation. The individual may feel betrayed by his own body for even having sexual parts and the feelings associated with them.

For the spouse: Feelings of "safety" may be mixed or hard to come by for the abused child—now an adult. There is usually a sense of having to be constantly vigilant and aware of her surroundings. Think of these children as "scared rabbits," always watching and waiting and ready to "flee" at a moment's notice. Trust doesn't come easily to someone in this state and may take years to establish.

In this atmosphere, physical and emotional intimacy can be extremely difficult for the adult survivor. They may experience flashbacks, anger, and use control as a way to keep themselves feeling "safe." This can often be hard on the spouse, who never knows what may trigger these feelings and emotions. One minute you may be enjoying a nice sexual experience and the next your spouse is curled into a fetal position and hiding in the closet! He may not even be able to express what is going on because he doesn't know himself.

The important thing to remember is that your spouse is injured—spiritually, emotionally, and perhaps physically. For example, if your spouse had a broken arm, that was never set properly, would you expect her to play tennis with you? No, you would encourage her to seek medical treatment so it could properly heal. However, even with a doctor's help, your spouse may never be able to play tennis with you in the way you want because the injury could have caused some irreparable damage. Just because you can't physically see your spouse's injury due to sexual abuse, it is there and it is real.

It is important for your spouse and you to seek counseling in order to "properly treat" the injury. Furthermore, just as re-breaking an incorrectly healed bone would cause great pain and require time for recovery, "re-breaking" the already broken soul will also cause emotional pain and require recovery. The good news is, with time, many of the symptoms associated with sexual abuse can be healed and put to rest. Many survivors learn how to quiet that scared rabbit and are able to have a healthy and functional relationship with their spouse and children. There is great hope.

For the survivor: You are not alone. This can't be repeated enough to survivors of sexual abuse. One of the greatest lies Satan perpetrates to sexually abused children is that they are alone, did something to bring on the abuse, and are not worthy of healthy and happy relationships. Children believe most things they are told, but you are no longer a child and have access to your adult brain. You have the opportunity to parent your "inner child" and gain a new perspective on the events of your life.

One of the first steps is to accept the reality of what happened and begin to discuss it. This takes great courage, but it allows that "child" to come out of the dark and begin to experience long-hoped-for light. There will be a grieving process over the loss of innocence and childhood. Just as you would feel compassion for someone who experienced the death of a loved one, showing compassion for yourself will allow you the opportunity to begin to nurture that "child."

It's important for you, your spouse, and your relationship that you seek proper care. It will be difficult and may feel overwhelming, but you are not the powerless child any longer. With support, time, and, most important, the Lord and His loving Atonement, you can experience peace. While there may be lingering scars, those injuries can be turned into strengths. The Lord didn't leave you alone then, and He won't leave you alone now.

Chapter Questions for Real-Life Application

1. Despite whatever challenges you may be experiencing, what is there in your life that uplifts you or brings you closer to God?

2. If you find yourself in one of these circumstances, do you have the support you need or do you find yourself feeling alone and needing more support?

3. If you need more support, what are the things preventing you from reaching out?

19

PROFESSIONAL HELP

Knowing when it may be time to seek additional help, what type of help is available, and how to find it

HAVE YOU EVER THOUGHT TO YOURSELF, "OUR PROBLEMS ARE not *that* bad. We don't need counseling!" It's common for us to see couples when problems have reached a breaking point in which one or both spouses feels an overwhelming hopelessness or despair. If a relationship is cruising along, and things aren't necessarily great, but they're not "that bad," counseling often doesn't enter the equation until slowly, over time, small problems become bigger and destructive to the relationship.

If you have ever trained for a running race, or known someone who has, you quickly find out there's a lot to learn, and preparation is a must. Successful runners seek assistance from others about nutrition, developing a training plan, and learning proper technique, and they talk with others who have run a race before. If you're injured—with a sprained ankle—you wouldn't expect to just keep running or not to seek medical help. Yet when it comes to our relationships, oftentimes we have the expectation we should know how to run the race and be a husband or wife. If we sustain an "injury," or have a festering problem, we think we should keep going and "run through it," which can create bigger problems.

Naturally, we learn our model for marriage and relationships from the circumstances in which we are raised. With the divorce rate reading approximately 50 percent, for both LDS and non-LDS, the expectation to "just know" how to have a healthy relationship, good communication, and functional intimacy is obviously unrealistic. We are okay with going to the doctor when we are sick or seeing a chiropractor when our back is out of alignment, and we are even comfortable with seeing these professionals for wellness check-ups. Unfortunately, getting repair work for our relationships tends to have a negative stigma attached.

But Our Relationship Is Pretty Good!

We had one reader who said, "I feel glad that my husband and I have been able to have really good communication about intimacy and are very open about it. Yet there are always areas we can improve. We have benefited from reading this book and taking some classes." Seeking tips for improvement doesn't require meeting with a therapist. It can mean picking up a book, reading it together, and learning new skills pertaining to an aspect of your relationship. Back to the running analogy, you both may be good runners, but you still learn something along the way that could improve your running or make your experience even more enjoyable. Many of you may have been living with an injury for so long that it has become your new "normal." You may have adapted in unhealthy ways to make up for the disruption of the injury.

Is Now the Time?

Some may be wondering: "Okay, so what is a healthy relationship? When should we seek out professional help?" Here are some circumstances requiring ecclesiastical, medical, or professional mental health help:

Mental, emotional, physical, spiritual, or sexual abuse is present.

Pain or ongoing physical discomfort is present during sex.

Something in your sexual or personal history is interfering with your ability to be intimate with your spouse.

Ongoing symptoms of depression or anxiety exist.

There is excessive or addictive use of pornography.

Unresolved shame or guilt is disrupting your relationship.

When It's Not Necessarily the Time

Here are some circumstances when you don't necessarily need to see a mental health therapist. They can happen to anyone, at any time, and can be a normal and healthy part of your sexual journey and experience together. Yet if any of these issues become disruptive to you or your relationship, causes anxiety or depression, or they occur on a regular basis, we recommend seeing a medical doctor or mental health professional.

The first time your penis goes flaccid during sex.

No matter how hard you try, the orgasm does not come.

You are almost "there" and you hear your baby cry and you have to start all over and figure it's too much work.

You are having sex and you achieve orgasm within thirty seconds.

The first time you think of a really handsome man while you are having sex with your husband.

You've had a baby and you do not feel like having sex at all.

You find someone of the same sex attractive.

You see your husband's face when he is on top of you and think, "I think I'm going to close my eyes."

Your children walk in on you during intimacy, and you think you've scarred them for life.

The bishop calls right after a "quickie" and wants to give you a new calling and you think, "He wouldn't be calling me if he knew what I just did."

Understanding the Available Resources

Under the umbrella of mental health providers are licensed clinical social workers, psychologists, marriage and family therapists, and licensed professional counselors, to name a few. Psychiatrists can also provide counseling but have the additional capacity to prescribe medication. These are licensed and regulated professionals with post-graduate education as well as substantial hours working under a supervisor.

The definition of psychotherapy is: "Any form of treatment for psychological, emotional, or behavior disorders in which a trained person establishes a relationship with one or several patients for the purpose of modifying or removing existing symptoms and promoting personality growth." If you have decided that you would benefit from mental-health therapy, finding a therapist can be a lot like dating to find the "one." Continue trying to find a therapist until you feel safe, understood, and are able to open up.

Coaching

Relationship coaching is geared toward improving a relatively healthy relationship in an objective, non-clinical way. It is results oriented and helps you attain the goals you identified. The coach provides skills, offers perspective, identifies disruptive habits and patterns, and provides a safe structure for mutual accountability.

Self-Help Books

There are many wonderful self-help books that can improve your relationship, increase your understanding, or teach new skills. It's important to consider the author's expertise or credentials, if there is an "agenda," and if it supports your personal, relational, and spiritual morals and values. See our resource section for some of the books we recommend.

Classes

There are many wonderful classes taught by LDS professionals. Be a proactive consumer and find out who is teaching the class, the teacher's method and approach, and the objective of the class. The First Presidency counseled against becoming involved with self-awareness groups that claim to be endorsed by the Church. While some classes or "retreats" may purport to provide quick solutions to problems, they can be harmful and undermine your spirituality and faith.

Medical Doctors

If you are experiencing sexual pain or discomfort, we recommend meeting with a physician. She may refer you to a specialist who has more knowledge about your condition. It's important not to delay seeking medical care if symptoms become disruptive.

Chapter Questions For Real-Life Application

1. Is discussing getting professional help a source of friction in your marriage? If so, refer to the chapter "Creating the Conversation" to help navigate a discussion.

2. If you are wanting professional help but your spouse is unwilling, what is preventing you from seeking help by yourself?

3. Have you had a negative experiencing with professional help? It may not be the professional help but the professional and it may take meeting with a few to find "the one." If you feel you need professional help but are hesitant, consider if a negative experience is contributing to this.

REAL RELATIONSHIP TIP!
A Cautionary Word on Quick Fixes

In 2001, The First Presidency had the following letter read in sacrament meeting:

> It has come to our attention that some commercial enterprises promising heightened self-esteem, improved family relationships, increased spirituality and the like by participating in their programs are implying Church endorsement. Such claims are untrue and unfounded.
>
> The Church has not endorsed any such enterprise. Neither should the Church's failure to formally challenge any such enterprise coming to its attention be construed as a tacit endorsement or stamp of approval.
>
> We repeat the counsel set forth in the Church Handbook of Instruction, page 157:
> "Church members should not participate in groups that:
> 1. Challenge religious and moral values or advocate unwarranted confrontation with spouse or family members as a means of reaching one's potential.

2. Imitate sacred rites or ceremonies.

3. Foster physical contact among participants.

4. Meet late into the evening or in the early-morning hours.

5. Encourage open confession or disclosure of personal information normally discussed only in confidential settings.

6. Cause a husband and wife to be paired with other parties."

We strongly counsel against affiliation with any such group and warn against believing any claim of Church approval, tacit or otherwise, by any private organization offering "experiential" or "empowerment" training.

Sincerely yours,

The First Presidency

Navigating the waters of "professional help" can be overwhelming and daunting when you are faced with understanding credentials and clinical "jargon." When a mental health issue presents itself, finding the most beneficial help can be challenging. Moreover, issues generally arise over the course of months, years, or a lifetime. Working through these difficulties takes commitment, letting go of poor coping habits, and learning new skills. Additionally, if you have undiagnosed mental health concerns, often these facilities do not conduct proper assessments or screenings, which can end up causing the individual greater harm. These facilities simply aren't equipped, or have the proper training or capacity to manage and treat most mental health issues. We echo the counsel of the First Presidency regarding these groups and offer additional things to consider when looking for professional help:

(1) Is the group or organization led by licensed mental health professionals?

(2) Do they supply adequate background about their services, intervention methods and leaders?

(3) Are they transparent with their practices?

(4) Are they offering being "cured" or "happy" in a short amount of time, such as a weekend?

If you answered no to the first three and yes to the last, we encourage you to avoid these centers. In Mosiah 4:27 it reads,

"And see that all these things are done in wisdom and order; for it is not requisite that a man should run faster than he has strength. And again, it is expedient that he should be diligent, that thereby he might win the prize; therefore, all things must be done in order."

True mental and emotional health doesn't come easily but is acquired by patience and persistence. Line upon line, precept upon precept.

AFTERWORD

Intimacy and Sexuality are wonderful, complicated, dynamic, and challenging aspects of life and relationships. Ed and Deb Shapiro say, "One of the great benefits of a loving relationship is that it provides a safe space for all of these fears that have never before seen the light of day to be acknowledged, known, and held. In other words, love brings up everything that isn't love." With this in mind, relationships face many trying times creating the mountain landscape we discussed and it's through the tender mercies of the Lord that we can endure and fight for our marriage, family, and meaningful intimacy.

Elder Bednar said in a talk,

The Lord's tender mercies are the very personal and individualized blessings, strength, protection, assurances, guidance, lovingkindness, consolation, support, and spiritual gifts which we receive from and because of and through the Lord Jesus Christ. Truly, the Lord suits his mercies according to the conditions of the children of men. As you and I face challenges and tests in our lives, the gift of faith and an appropriate sense of personal confidence that reaches beyond our own capacity are two examples of the tender mercies of the Lord. Repentance and forgiveness of sins and peace of conscience are examples of the tender mercies of the Lord. And the persistence and the fortitude that enable us to press forward with cheerfulness through physical limitations and spiritual difficulties are examples of the tender mercies of the Lord. (Bednar 2)

May you all find the joy in the work, the strength in commitment and the hope of a relationship that is meaningful and intimate.

RESOURCES

THESE ARE SOME OF OUR FAVORITE WEBSITES AND BOOKS WE recommend most often. For a current list of resources, books, blogs, websites, therapists, and more, visit our website at www .RealIntimacyBook.com

Depression

Reaching For Hope: An LDS Perspective on Recovering From Depression by Meghan Decker

Feeling Good by David Burns

Homosexuality

Goodbye, I Love You by Carol Lynn Pearson

In Quiet Desperation by Fred & Marilyn Matis, Ty Mansfield

No More Goodbyes: Circling the Wagons Around Our Gay Loved Ones by Carol Lynn Pearson

Infertility

Love and Infertility: Survival Strategies for Balancing Infertility, Marriage and Life by Kristin Magnacca

Infertility: Help, Hope, Healing by Kerstin Daynes

www.LDSInfertility.org

www.Resolve.org

Infidelity

After the Affair: Healing the Pain and Rebuilding Trust when a Partner Has Been Unfaithful by Janis Abrahms Spring

Intimacy after a Baby

And Baby Makes Three: A Six Step Program For Preserving Marital Intimacy and Rekindling Romance After the Baby Arrives by John M. Gottman and Julie Schwartz Gottman

Marriage Prep

Saving Your Marriage Before It Starts: Seven Questions to Ask Before and After You Marry by Les Parrot III, Leslie Parrot

Mormon Culture

DaughtersofMormonism.blogspot.com

www.MormonStories.org

MormonTherapist.blogspot.com

www.ModernMormonMen.com

www.TheCulturalHallPodcast.com

Pornography and Sexual Addiction

Out of the Shadows: Understanding Sexual Addiction by Patrick Carnes

Your Sexually Addicted Spouse by Barbara Steffens and Marsha Means

Confronting Pornography: A Guide to Prevention and Recovery for Individuals, Loved Ones and Leaders by Mark D. Chamberlain, Daniel D. Gray, and Rory C. Reid

www.LifeStarNetwork.org

www.SonsOfHelaman.org

Postpartum Depression

Life Will Never Be the Same: The Real Mom's Postpartum Survival Guide by Ann L. Dunwold, Diane G. Sanford

What am I Thinking? Having a Baby After Postpartum Depression by Karen Kleiman

Down Came the Rain by Brooke Shields

www.TheHealingGroup.com

www.Postpartum.net

www.PostpartumProgress.org

Pregnancy

The Girlfriends Guide to Pregnancy by Vicki Iovine

Pregnancy, Childbirth and the Newborn: The Complete Guide by Penny Simkin, Janet Whalley, Ann Kepler

Birthing From Within: An Extra-Ordinary Guide to Childbirth Preparation by Pam England, Rob Horowitz

Relationships and Intimacy

Starved Stuff: Feeding The 7 Basic Needs of Healthy Relationships by Matt Townsend

Hold Me Tight: Seven Conversations For Lifetime of Love by Susan Johnson

The Dance of Intimacy by Harriet G. Lerner

Getting The Love You Want: A Guide for Couples by Harville Hendrix

The Intimacy Factor by Pia Mellody

The Five Love Languages by Dr. Chapman

The Seven Principles for Making Marriage Work by John Gottman

Take Back Your Marriage by William Doherty

The Divorce Remedy by Michele Weiner-Davis

This Is Your Brain In Love: New Scientific Breakthroughs for a More Passionate and Emotionally Healthy Relationship by Earl Henslin

Self-Esteem

Confronting The Myth of Self-Esteem: 12 Keys to Finding Peace by Ester Rasband

The Gifts of Imperfection: Let Go of Who You Think You Are Supposed to Be and Embrace Who You Are by Brene Brown

The Self-Esteem Guided Journal: A 10-week Program by Matthew McKay, PhD & Catharine Sutker

Sex

The Sex Starved Marriage: Boosting Your Marriage Libido, A Guide For Couples by Michele Davis Weiner

Mating in Captivity: Unlocking Erotic Intelligence by Esther Perel

And They Were Not Ashamed: Strengthening Marriage Through Sexual Fulfillment by Laura Brotherson

365 Days: A Memoir of Intimacy by Charla Mueller, Betsy Thorpe

Passionate Marriage: Keeping Love and Intimacy Alive in Committed Relationships by David Schnarch

The Magic of Sex by Miriam Stoppard

The Elusive Orgasm: A Woman's Guide to Why She Can't and How She Can Orgasm by Vivenne Cass

Sexual Abuse

The Courage to Heal: A Guide for Women Survivors of Sexual Abuse by Ellen Bass, Laura Davis

Sexual Problems

Sexual Healing: The Completest Guide For Overcoming Sexual Problems by Barbara Keesling

Healing Painful Sex: A Woman's Guide to Confronting, Diagnosing, and Treating Sexual Pain by Deborah Coady, Nancy Fish

Resurrecting Sex: Resolving Sexual Problems and Rejuvenating Your Relationship by David Schnarch

When Sex Hurts: A Woman's Guide to Banishing Sexual Pain by Andrew Goldstein, Caroline Pukall, Irwin Goldstein

Coping with Erectile Dysfunction by Metz and McCarthy

Coping with Premature Ejaculation by Metz and McCarthy

Kristin B. Hodson and Thomas G. Harrison offer counseling in Salt Lake City, Utah over the phone and through Skype. Alisha Worthington provides classes and seminars in Salt Lake City as well as on the phone and online. You can find out more by visiting:

www.RealIntimacyBook.com or www.TheHealingGroup.com

BIBLIOGRAPHY

Asay, Carlos E. "Flaxen Threads." Brigham Young University. LDS Fireside. Brigham Young University, Provo, UT. 7 Feb. 1982.

Bednar, David A. "The Tender Mercies of the Lord," *New Era*, Feb. 2012, 2.

Brotherson, L. M. *And They Were Not Ashamed: Strengthening Marriage Through Sexual Fulfillment*. Boise, ID: Inspire Book, 2004.

Centers for Disease Control. 2002. http://www.cdc.gov/nchs/fastats/fertile.htm.

Cloud, H, & J. Townsend. *Boundaries: When To Say Yes, When To Say No*. Grand Rapids, MI: Zondervan, 1992.

Cohen, S. J. *Holy Letter: A Study In Jewish Sexual Morality*. New York City: Jason Aronson, 1994.

Dalton, Elaine S. "He Knows You by Name." *Ensign*, 2005.

Daynes, K. *Infertility: Help, Hope and Healing*. Springville, UT: Cedar Fort, 2010.

Economy Watch "Porn Industry, Porn Trade, Adult Entertainment." Economy Watch 30 Jun. 2010. http://www.economywatch.com/world-industries/porn-industry.html.

"Female Orgasms: Myths and Facts." SOGC. 4 May. 2011. http://www.sogc.org/health/health-myths_e.asp.

Finlayson-Fife, J. (2010, Dec. 2). "LDS Female Sexuality." Mormon Stories Podcast by John Dehlin 214–216 from http://mormonstories.org/214-216-lds-female-sexuality-with-dr-jennifer-finlayson-fife/.

Frost, Robert. "Frost, Mending Wall." http://writing.upenn.edu/~afilreis/88/frost-mending.html. 18 Jul. 2007. 13 Oct. 2011. http://writing.upenn.edu/~afilreis/88/frost-mending.html.

Get The Facts. Postpartum Support International from http://postpartum.net/Get-the-Facts.aspx.

Goldberg, Ellen H, and M. Adinolfi, and U. Wiberg, and H. Sharma. "H-Y Antigen and Sex Determination [and Discussion]." Philosophical Transactions of the Royal Society of London 322 (1988): 73-81. http://www.jstor.org/discover/10.2307/2396849?uid=3739928&uid=2129&uid=2&uid=70&uid=4&uid=3739256&sid=55953350743.

Good Girl Syndrome Part I and II. Daughters of Mormonism 30 & 31 from www.daughtersofmormonism.blogspot.com.

Gray, D, & R. Reid. *Confronting Pornography*. Salt Lake City, UT: Deseret Book, 2005.

Henslin, Earl. *This is Your Brain in Love: New Scientific Breakthroughs for a More Passionate and Emotionally Healthy Marriage*. Nashville, TN: Thomas Nelon, 2009.

Hope, T. P. "Your Nest Is Empty? Enjoy Each Other." *New York Times*, Jan. 19, 2009.

Human Sexual Behavior. Magnus Hirschfeld Archive for Sexology from http://www2.hu-berlin.de/sexology/ATLAS_EN/html/human_sexual_behavior.html.

Leaf, D. *Who Switched Off Your Brain: Solving the Mystery of He Said/ She Said*. Nashville, TN: Thomas Nelson, 2011.

Love, P. *The Truth About Love*. New York City: Fireside, 2001.

Magnacca, K. *Love and Infertility: Strategies For Balancing Infertility, Marriage and Life*. Washington D.C.: Lifeline Press, 2004.

Maxwell, N. A. "Remember How Merciful The Lord Hath Been." *Ensign*, 2004.

Mellody, Pia, and Lawrence Freundlich. *The Intimacy Factor: The Ground Rules for Overcoming the Obstacles to Truth, Respect, and Lasting Love*. New York City: Harper Collins, 2004.

Monson, T. S. "The Master's Blueprint." *Ensign*, 2006.

Morris, D. *Intimate Behavior: A Zoologist's Classic Study of Human Intimacy*. New York City: Kodansha America Inc., 1997.

National Center for Health Statistics. Divison of Vital Statistics. Demarius V. Miller and Laura Drescher, CDC/NCHM/Division of Creative Births, marriages, divorces, and deaths: Provisional data for 2009. 27 Aug. 2009. http://www.cdc.gov/nchs/data/nvsr/nvsr58/nvsr58_25.pdf.

Parker, N. H. "The Mormon Therapist" from mormontherapist. blogspot.com.

Reese, Michael, and Debby Herbernick, and J. Dennis Fortenberry, and Brian Dodge, and Stephanie Sanders, and Vanessa Schick. "National Survey of Sexual Health and Behavior." *The Journal of Sexual Medicine*: Center for Sexual Health Promotion, Bloomingron, 2010.

Sellers, T. S. Tina Schermer Sellers, M.S. from www.tinaschermer-sellers.com.

Shakespeare, W. *Hamlet*. New York City: Simon & Brown, 2011.

Shapiro, Ed and Deb. "Intimacy: Into Me I See—Into Me You See!" *Huffpost Healthy Living*, June 8, 2010.

Steffens Phd, LPCC, Barbara, and Marsha Means, MA. *Your Sexually Addicted Spouse.* Far Hills: New Horizon Press, 2009.

Stoppard, D. *The Magic of Sex.* New York City: DK Publishing. 1991.

Story, Louise "Anywhere the Eye Can See, It's Likely to See an Ad." *New York Times,* 15 Jan. 2007.

The Kinsey Institute for Research in Sex, Gender and Reproduction. Bloomington, Indiana. http://www.kinseyinstitute.org/.

Thomas, G. L. *Sacred Marriage.* Grand Rapids, MI: Zondervan, 2009.

Weiner Davis, M. *The Sex-Starved Marriage.* New York City: Simon & Schuster, 2003.

Weiner Davis, M. *The Sex-Starved Wife: What To Do When He Has Lost Desire.* New York City: Simon & Schuster, 2008.

www.LDS.org. 2012. http://www.lds.org/handbook/handbook-2-administering-the-church/selected-church-policies?lang=eng&query=unnatural#21.4.5.

ABOUT THE AUTHORS

Kristin B. Hodson, LCSW

Kristin graduated from Brigham Young University—Hawaii in 2003 with a degree in social work with an international emphasis. In 2006, she graduated from the University of Utah with a masters degree in social work with clinical and medical emphasis. She has worked as a psychotherapist since 2006, and in 2009 she opened a mental health clinic in Holladay, Utah, specializing in women's mental health. She regularly presents at various universities and to community groups on relationships, pregnancy, and postpartum mental health, as well as finding balance and wellness in everyday living. She has a passion for women's mental health and human and relational sexuality and spirituality. She finds her greatest joy in pursuing life's adventures alongside her husband and two children.

Alisha B. Worthington, SSW

Alisha graduated from Brigham Young University with a degree in social work, and she works part time for The Healing Group—a therapeutic clinic. She is a marital intimacy coach, helping couples and individuals in their quest for greater intimacy. Since 2008 she has worked as a freelance writer providing articles for websites on topics such as parenting, dentistry, prisons, dating, and so on. She contributes to her community by speaking to groups and holding educational forums. Alisha has a passion for women's issues, pregnancy and birth, and education. She has been married fifteen years and is the mother of seven children. She feels this fact alone qualifies her to write a book on marital intimacy since she and her husband have continued to experience great intimacy!

Thomas G. Harrison, LCSW

Thom has been practicing in Utah with a clinical license since 1977. He has taught at the University of Utah medical school, the graduate school of social work, and the law school since 1977. He has taught and spoken to many groups on human sexuality and sexuality within relationships. He has counseled over three thousand survivors of sexual abuse. He has been trained in cognitive behavioral therapy, psychodynamic therapy, reality-oriented therapy, and relationship therapy. Harrison has a successful practice in Salt Lake City, Utah, and counsels individuals, couples, and families.